Fluid Modernity

Fluid Modernity offers an innovative, encompassing, historical grasp of the politics of water in the Middle East in the context of modern capitalism and world politics. Drawing upon conceptions of power by Foucault and Agamben, it examines how water, through its modern capitalist production, is transformed into a water apparatus that binds people to power. In trans-boundary watercourses, states get involved in the formation of international governmentalities. The book revisits the history of fluid modernity in the Middle East from late Ottoman times to the present. It focuses on water conflict and cooperation between states (Israel and Arab states and Turkey, Syria and Iraq), on state policies towards subaltern subjects (Israel and Turkey in relation to Palestinians and Kurds, respectively) and on the water politics of rebellious movements. After a conceptual chapter discussing fluid modernity, the book traces water politics in the region in a diachronic perspective. It explores how water diplomacy, infrastructure loans, reservoir construction, discourses of sovereignty and conflict have weighed on the development of governance and governmentality in the region.

Fluid Modernity will be of great interest to postgraduates, researchers, academics and intellectuals interested in Middle East Studies, Hydropolitics, Water and Society, Geopolitics, Political Theory, Resistance as well as to NGOs dealing with water.

Gilberto Conde is Professor at the Center for Asia and Africa Studies of El Colegio de México, where he teaches Geography and History of the Middle East and North Africa, and works on Arab, Turkish and Kurdish politics and society with a special interest on authoritarianism, rebellion, geopolitics, capitalism and water. Before joining El Colegio de México in 2011, he taught world history and critical geopolitics in Tijuana at Universidad Autónoma de Baja California, and carried out research on water and society at El Colegio de la Frontera Norte. Having lived in Syria, Tunisia and Turkey for several years and travelled extensively in the Middle East and North Africa, Gilberto is keen to bring a Latin American, non-West, decolonial approach to his work. He edited *Estudios de Asia y África*, the oldest Latin American journal on the non-Latin American Global South, from 2012 through 2016. He has published several authored or edited volumes on the Middle East as well as numerous journal articles and book chapters.

Routledge Focus on Modern Subjects
Series Editor: **Saurabh Dube**, Professor-Researcher,
Distinguished Category, El Colegio de México

Routledge Focus on Modern Subjects has a broad yet particular purpose. It explores quotidian claims made on the *modern*—understood as idea and image, practice and procedure—as part of everyday articulations of modernity in South Asia, Africa, and the Middle East. Here, the category-entity of the subject refers not only to social actors who have been active participants in historical processes of modernity, but as equally implying branch of learning and area of study, topic and theme, question and matter, and issue and business. Our effort is to explore such modern subjects in a range of distinct yet overlaying ways.

The titles in the series address earlier understandings of the modern and recent reconsiderations of modernity by focusing on a clutch of common and critical questions. Indeed, our bid is to carefully query aggrandizing representations of modernity "as" the West, while prudently tracking the place of such projections in the commonplace unravelling of the modern in Global Souths today.

Books in this series

The Dazzle of the Digital
Unbundling India Online
Meghna Bal and Vivan Sharan

Disciplines of Modernity
Archives, Histories, Anthropologies
Saurabh Dube

Fluid Modernity
The Politics of Water in the Middle East
Gilberto Conde

For more information about this series, please visit: www.routledge.com/Routledge-Focus-on-Modern-Subjects/book-series/RFOMS

Fluid Modernity

The Politics of Water in the Middle East

Gilberto Conde

R Routledge
Taylor & Francis Group

LONDON AND NEW YORK

First published 2023
by Routledge
2 Park Square, Milton Park, Abingdon, Oxon OX14 4RN

and by Routledge
605 Third Avenue, New York, NY 10158

Routledge is an imprint of the Taylor & Francis Group, an information business

© 2023 Gilberto Conde

British Library Cataloguing-in-Publication Data
A catalogue record for this book is available from the British Library

ISBN: 978-1-032-41225-2 (hbk)
ISBN: 978-1-032-41226-9 (pbk)
ISBN: 978-1-003-35690-5 (ebk)

DOI: 10.4324/9781003356905

Typeset in Times New Roman
by Newgen Publishing UK

To Clara and Leyla

Contents

Maps

Series editor's statement

Saurabh Dube

Routledge Focus on Modern Subjects has a broad yet particular purpose. It seeks to explore quotidian claims made on the *modern*—understood as idea and image, practice and procedure—as part of everyday articulations of modernity in South Asia, the Middle East, and Africa. Here, the category-entity of the *subject* also has wide purchase. It refers not only to social actors who have been active participants in historical processes of modernity, but equally implies branch of learning and area of study, topic and theme, question and matter, and issue and business. The series attempts to address such modern subjects in a range of distinct yet overlaying ways.

Questions of modernity have always been bound to issues of being/becoming modern. These themes have been discussed in various ways for long now.[1] For convenience, we might distinguish between two broad, opposed tendencies. On the one hand, over the past few centuries, it is the West/Europe that has been seen as the locus and the habitus of the modern and modernity. Such a West is imaginary yet tangible, principally envisioned in the image of the North Atlantic world. And it is from these arenas that modernity and the modern appear as spreading outwards to transform other, distant and marginal, peoples in the mold and the wake of the West. On the other hand, such propositions have been contested by rival claims, including especially from within Romanticist and anti-modernist dispositions. Here, if the modern and modernity have been often understood as intimating the fundamental fall of humanity, everywhere, so too have the aggrandizements of an analytical reason been countered through procedures of a hermeneutic provenance.

Needless to say, these contending tendencies have for long each found imaginative articulations, and I provide indicative examples from our own times. The work of philosophers such as Jürgen Habermas and Charles Taylor and historians such as Reinhart Koselleck and Hans Ulrich Gumbrecht have opened up the exact terms, textures, and transformations of modernity and the modern. At the same time, they have arguably located the constitutive conditions of these phenomena in Western Europe and Euro-America. In contrast, anti-modernist sensibilities have found innovative elaborations in, say, the "critical traditionalism" of Ashis Nandy in South Asia; and the querying of Eurocentric thought has been intriguingly expressed by the scholars of the "coloniality of knowledge" and "decoloniality of power" in Latin America. These powerful positions variously rest on assumptions of innocence before and outside Europe and the West, modernity and the modern.

Engaging with yet going beyond such prior emphases, recent work on modernity has charted new directions, departures that have served to foreground questions of modernity in academic agendas and on intellectual horizons, more broadly. I indicate four critical trends. First and foremost, there have been works focusing on different expressions of the modern and distinct articulations of modernity as historically grounded and/or culturally expressed, articulations that query *a priori* projections and sociological formalisms underpinning the category-entity. Second, there are the studies that have diversely explored issues of "early" and "colonial" and "multiple" and "alternative" modernity/ modernities. Third, we find imaginative ethnographic, historical, and theoretical explorations of modernity's conceptual cognates such as globalization, capitalism, and cosmopolitanism as well as of attendant issues of state, nation, and democracy. Fourth and finally, there have been varied explorations of the enchantments of modernity and of the magic of the modern, understood not as analytical errors but as formative of social worlds. These studies have ranged from the elaborations of the fetish of the state, the sacred character of modern sovereignty, the uncanny of capitalism, and the routine enticements of modernity through to the secular magic of representational practices such as entertainment shows, cinema, and advertising.

Routledge Focus on Modern Subjects engages and exceeds, takes forward and departs from such concerns in its own manner. To start off, its titles address the queries and concepts entailed in earlier explorations of the modern and recent reconsiderations of modernity by focusing on a clutch of common and critical questions. These issues turn on the everyday elaborations of the modern, the quotidian configurations of modernity, on the Indian subcontinent. Next, rather than simply asserting the empirical plurality of modernity and the modern, the series approaches the routine, even banal, expressions of the modern as registering contingency, contradiction, and contention as lying at the core of modernity. Further, it only follows that our bid is not to indolently exorcize aggrandizing representations of modernity *as* the West, but to prudently track instead the play of such projections in the commonplace unraveling of the modern in Global Souths today. Finally, such procedures not only recast broad questions—for instance of cosmopolitanism and globalization, state and citizenship, Eurocentrism and Nativism, aesthetics and authority—by approaching them through routine renderings of the modern in contemporary worlds. They also stay with the dense, exact expressions of modernity yet all the while attending to their larger, critical implications, prudently thinking *both* down to the ground.

In keeping with the spirit of the series, all its titles stand informed by specific renderings—as well as focused rethinking—of key categories and processes. Two exact instances. In different ways, concepts and processes of power and politics alongside those of community and identity variously run through the *Routledge Focus on Modern Subjects.* Here, neither power nor politics are rendered as signifying solely institutional relations of authority centering on the state and its subjects. Rather, the bid is to articulate these as equally embodying diffuse domains and intimate arrangements of authority and desire, including their seductions and subversions. Actually, as parts of such force-fields, state and government, their policy and program might now assume twinned dimensions in understandings of modern subjects. Here can be found densely embodied disciplinary techniques toward forming and transforming subjects-citizens, where such protocols and their reworking by citizens-subjects no less register the shaping of authority by anxiety, uncertainty, and alterity, of the structuring of command by deferral, difference, and displacement.

At the same time, the series approaches community and identity as modern processes of meaning and authority, located at core of nation and globalization. This is to say that instead of approaching identity and community as already given entities that are principally antithetical to modernity, this cluster explores communities and identities as wide-ranging processes of formations of subjects, expressing collective groupings and particular personhoods. Defined within social relationships of production and reproduction, appropriation and approbation, and power and difference, emergent identities, cultural communities, and their mutations appear now as essential elements in the quotidian constitution, expressions, and transformations of modern subjects.

The work

Fluid Modernity (henceforth, *FM*) ably articulates our aim to widen the address of modernity and its subjects. On the one hand, the book expands the focus on South Asia of the first four titles in the series, extending the locus to the Middle Eastern world. On the other hand, Gilberto Conde seizes upon a distinct modern subject that is also a subject of modernity: Water, its plural politics and expressions, its key containments and impulses, its many moods and demands, its discrete desires and despairs. Together, it is the conjunction of these double imperatives that exemplify the fit between *FM* and *Routledge Focus on Modern Subjects*, especially the wider keenness of this series to stay with and think through critical heterogeneity—searching and groping outside the box.

Imaginatively, Conde accesses and exceeds familiar terms of "hydro-politics" through detailed textures of "hegemony." Here, the readily "technological" is shot through with the formatively "social; "water apparatuses" shored up by "governmental reasons"; and noisy clamors of statist sovereignty are broken upon by unruly specters of recalci-trant subalterns. Now the "dialectic of the Enlightenment" finds newer renderings through "biopolitics/biopower", each marked by "states/spaces" of "emergency/exception." In these fluid terrains, Theodor Adorno and Max Horkheimer, Michel Foucault and Giorgio Agamben, Antonio Gramsci and Edward Said, all rub shoulders with one another, as they do also with many, many other interlocutors.

All this is impressive accomplishment. Yet I have chosen not to write about the theoretical formations and methodological formulations at stake in *FM*. The reason is simple. I know little about the eddies and flows, the depths and surfaces, the currents and turbulences of water as substance and subject, at once subaltern and sovereign. And so, rather than writing the usual Foreword to the volumes in this series, I offer only this short statement, leaving the reader to navigate and chart the course ahead.

Note

1 The discussion in this Statement of different understandings of modernity (and the modern) draws upon a wide range of scholarship. Instead of cluttering the short piece with numerous references, indicated here are a few of my works that have addressed these themes – in dialogue with relevant literatures – and that back the claims made ahead. Needless to say, prior arguments and emphases are being cryptically condensed and radically

rearranged for the present purposes. Saurabh Dube, *Subjects of Modernity: Time/Space, Disciplines, Margins* (Manchester: Manchester University Press, 2017); Saurabh Dube, *Stitches on Time: Colonial Textures and Postcolonial Tangles* (Durham and London: Duke University Press, 2004); and Saurabh Dube, *Disciplines of Modernity: Archives, Histories, Anthropologies* (London and New Delhi: Routledge, forthcoming 2022). Consider also, Saurabh Dube, *After Conversion: Cultural Histories of Modern India* (New Delhi: Yoda Press, 2010), Saurabh Dube (ed.), *Enchantments of Modernity: Empire, Nation, Globalization* (New Delhi and London: Routledge, 2009, 2010); and Saurabh Dube (ed.), *Handbook of Modernity in South Asia: Modern Makeovers* (New Delhi: Oxford University Press, 2011).

Preface

One of the things that first impressed me when I began travelling to the Middle East and North Africa was the relation of people to water. In Casablanca, Cairo or Istanbul, you could see water fountains everywhere or water being made available for others to drink freely, and often many people unknown to each other would share the same glass or flask by drinking in such way as to avoid touching the rim with their lips. Eventually, I decided to study the region and to devote much of my time to reflecting on politics in relation to water and large dams. The region was famous not only for its conflicts, but also for its aridity. I only hope that colleagues and activists find my inquiries helpful, suggestive.

In preparing the book, I conducted fieldwork in different parts of Turkey, Syria and Iraq, as well as in Jordan and Israel-Palestine. Visits were done to the three first countries during two distinct periods: from the summer of 2000 to the end of 2003 and during the summer of 2013. Two short visits were also made to Jordan, one in 2017 and another in 2019, and one to Israel-Palestine in autumn 2019. Scholars, librarians, activists, citizens of different religious, ethnic and political affiliations, affected by and affecting water policies, as well as government officials, were formally or casually interviewed. Ideas, materials, information and impressions obtained from and through them, were invaluable in shaping my own. Only modestly can my debt and gratitude to all of them be expressed here. I also want to acknowledge the material support of two Mexican funds that supported my research activities, the El Colegio de México Fondo de Apoyo Colmex a la Investigación (FACI), from 2019 to 2020, and the Mexican Ministry of Public Education (SEP) Programa de Mejoramiento del Profesorado (PROMEP), from 2012 to 2013.

Many have knowingly or unknowingly contributed to this book. The list is long and many names are missing, including kind and lovely people in Turkey, Syria, Iraq, Kurdistan, Isreal/Palestine, Jordan, Lebanon. My apologies to them. Saurabh Dube and Ishita Banerjee have supported me through the years, providing important ideas and always helping renew my ways of grasping the world. Mentors, colleagues, students and friends, Gilbert Achcar, Enzo Traverso, Rubén Chuaqui, Munif Mulkhim, Randa Baas, Carmen Arriola, Luis Aboites, Edith Kauffer, Harlan Koff, Carmen Maganda, Azize Aslan, Masis Kürkçügil, Koray Çalişkan, Zeynep Çatay, Azad Pirdaoud, Seda Altug, Michael Provence, Talal Rizq, Ziyad Ayoub Arbach, Rocío Rojas, Carli Pierson, Hamid Abud Russell. Sebastián Estremo, Verónica Souto, knowingly or not, have all offered invaluable insights that are reflected variously in this book. A special expression of gratitude goes to Dr. El-Zaim, who passed away in December 2007. Much of the research for this book I did with his direct support. I also want to thank Iraís Fuentes, who has given me not only invaluable help with the maps, but also with intellectual input as student, colleague and friend that has contributed to the development of the theoretical inquires explored in this text. I also want to thank Danny Laird, who patiently listened to me when I started conceiving the book and graciously accepted to read it and get rid of some of its clumsiness. Andrew McLaren was also incredibly helpful in this respect. The usual disclaimers as to their innocence in relation to the failures of the book are of course due, as they are of my exclusive responsibility.

As for the transliteration of Arabic and other non-Latin scripts, I have sought to use what seemed to me the most intuitive method. Names are usually written in the most common ways found in the English press or academic publications. Whenever possible, I avoid using diacritics, as, alas, they seem to cause more confusion than anything else among non-specialists.

Glossary of concepts

For a more comprehensive explanation of these concepts, please refer to Chapter 1.

Bipolitics, bipower. In the Foucauldian conception of power, modern states and societies tend to exercise power and politics through the administration of life, as shepherds manage the lives of their flocks, rather than death, as was the case in premodern societies. Reflecting on the concept, Agamben (1998, 2005) concludes that biopolitics includes its contrary, **thanatopolitics**, as it actually administers both life and death. Traverso (2012, 206–209) concludes that biopolitics is about the administration of life in normal times, but during crises modern states can unleash killing machines much more lethal than those of the past. It should be kept in mind that, as Walter Benjamin (1989) reminds us, for the oppressed, "the 'state of emergency' in which we live is not the exception but the rule". This book concurs. Biopower is the administration of life, of populations, but when the powerful find themselves in a crisis, they can decree **states of emergency** and **spaces of exception** in which they discriminate and administer life and death.

Fluid Modernity. In the last two centuries, water use and infrastructure have been developing more rapidly than before. Distribution of water has been thoroughly transformed, increasing both in amounts and forms of access. This has influenced social interactions and culture, which have radically changed to a point in which societies view the new forms of accessing water as natural. Without really thinking about it, people have become dependent on states and utilities companies that manage the resource and its distribution. Fluid modernity also has involved turning water and its infrastructure into commodities.

Full-fledged fluid modernity. Since the 20th century, the pace and complexity of dam building has accelerated so much that one or more reservoirs hamper the flow of every significant river in the world. Entire development programmes are often built around dams. Coupled with a boost in water utilisation in agriculture, industry, cities and households, these transformations have numerous social and political implications.

Governmental reason and governmentality. Within the Foucauldian idea of biopower, the governmental reason, also called governmentality, is the apparatus system that administers life in modern societies, binding state and subjects in subtle ways. More than through policing or violence, individuals and social groups are disciplined and discipline themselves by being part of governmentality. The governmental reason operates on the bases of a series of parallel but overlapping apparatuses.

International governmental reason. Strong states seek to replicate on the international or regional scale what seems to work so well within states in ensuring the exercise of power over individuals and societies. It is always more effective to have the subaltern discipline themselves than having to force them into compliance. Both the mechanisms of governmentality, domestic and international, are invoked in the exercise of international power.

State of emergency, state of exception. See "Biopolitics".

Space of exception. See "Biopolitics".

Thanatopolitics. See "Biopolitics".

Watar apparatus or dispositif. Apparatuses, the building blocks of the governmental reason, are constituted by discursive, material and practical elements that help in administering life. The **water apparatus**—formed by dams, aqueducts, water distribution networks and their administration, nationalist discourses on water and the mere availability of the fluid in countless forms—runs parallel to and overlaps other dispositifs (such as the security apparatus). Collectively they constitute the governmental reason. Strong states have sought to develop **international water apparatuses**, not always successfully, to help them mobilise an international biopower through the establishment of an international governmental reason.

Introduction

Get up, open the tap, fill the kettle, eat some fruit, butter and bread, have some yoghurt, open the tap again, wash the dishes, go to the toilet, open the tap, wash, flush, take a shower, put on your clothes, move on. Thirsty while on the go? Buy a bottle if you can afford it. God wants you to make it available to the thirsty? Not a problem, have factory sealed cups under a pile of ice cubes so that passers-by can fetch one and quench their thirst. Who really thinks about water and what it takes to make it available in such easy forms? Water is conveniently delivered to millions, billions, through often invisible pipes, and mysteriously disposed of through even better disguised drainage systems. Though unevenly distributed, water availability today cannot be compared to that of the past. The intricate facilities necessary to make this magic come true are constitutive of the governmental reason. As thinking about water complexities withers away among most people, as the state and utilities companies go through literally unimaginable troubles to make such an essential matter of life easily available, people become bound to power, subjects of a modern water power, fluid modernity, through the establishment of water apparatuses.

Certainly, dams and pipelines are truly astonishing pieces of engineering, and the lakes created by them are fantastic. I can attest to it personally. When I was a kid, my father used to take my siblings and me to Abelardo L. Rodríguez Dam near Tijuana, Mexico, for weekend picnics. In a summer spent in the United States at age 12, I was taken for Saturday outings to Stevens Creek Reservoir to swim and then for a road trip to Glen Canyon Dam, where we camped on the shores of Lake Powell. Beyond awe and leisure, dams and their lakes allow for hydropower generation, irrigation, flood control, aquaculture and tourism regardless of when precipitation takes place. Perhaps as importantly, dam-building itself has played a role in economics. Post-Second World

DOI: 10.4324/9781003356905-1

War state investments in infrastructure partially explain the economic boom of the 1950s and 1960s.

Reservoirs and other water development technology are radical "human" interventions in "nature". The use of inverted commas here should not be taken lightly. One could replace the word "human" with "state" or "business" as well as "nature" with "what used to be nature" or "what used to be agricultural lands" to be more accurate. Dams, particularly large ones, fragment space, change landscapes, transform ecosystems, and allow for the management and control of populations. They are biopolitics, usually deployed without giving much thought to life itself, but in a very narrow sense.

Reservoirs and pipelines are noteworthy for an awkward part of their functionality, which has become clear in the Middle East since the mid-20th century. Besides their stated purposes, they constitute strategic structures in times of conflict or even war, which sadly often has been the case in the region for a century or so. In international watercourses, they are the subject of high—and low—diplomacy and politics. While in 2000 it was possible to cross al-Thawra Dam in Syria under surveillance, and in 2013 one could rather freely visit Dukan Dam in Iraqi Kurdistan, it was still forbidden for a foreigner even to approach Atatürk Dam unless accompanied by authorised Turkish state officials. Take, for example, the Renaissance Dam in Ethiopia. The reservoir is an important project for the state, for economic partners and political associates. Besides being an important business opportunity, it also helps developing the water apparatus, which helps strengthening the governmental reason within the country. The dam, however, has multiple consequences, as it affects the downstream riparian neighbours of Ethiopia, let alone local populations and the environment.

Water infrastructure has been the stake of what has been called hydropolitics or even hydro-hegemony. Complex power relations have developed in connection to trans-boundary rivers and aquifers in the region. It seems clear that overall political interactions and circumstances, economic interests and power objectives determine when states hold a more aggressive or cooperative water relationship. In the domestic arena, the power asymmetry between state and populations is greater than among states in either the regional or the broader international context. In the Middle East, the postcolonial order contains a plainly colonial element over Palestinians and over Kurds. As will be argued, states have deployed over these peoples forms of internal biopolitics, which seem more like thanatopolitics.

Fluid modernity has developed in the Middle East at least since the end of the 19th century but has taken on a wholly new dimension in the second half of the 20th century. The United States and the Western Bloc intervened with important water diplomacy initiatives with multiple goals, including economic ones, of course, but especially aiming at political objectives. From then on, many dams, including some very large ones, and other water infrastructure were built, influencing interstate power relations and affecting people and nature. Fluid modernity involves political initiatives by strong states within and across borders, but weaker states and the subalterns become active subjects that often deploy strategies to limit, oppose or circumvent the water apparatus established by the strongest.

This book discusses water politics in a light different from that of classical and even critical hydropolitics, which seems to get its name from an analogy with geopolitics, with which it shares some of the crucial debates over a shorter span of time. First used by John Waterbury in his famous 1979 book on the Nile, a few efforts have been made to define it. In line with a large part of the hydropolitics scholarship until the second half of the 1990s, which may be called classical, Elhance (1997) considered it a discipline dealing with conflict and cooperation among states sharing a transboundary watercourse. Five years later, Turton (2002) proposed a different definition focusing on value and called for the incorporation of all sorts of scales, from the body and the town all the way to the international, and to unbind the breadth of issues covered. During the 2000s, authors developed what has been called critical hydropolitics theory, reflecting on water in relation to the legitimacy of power, state and nation (including Sneddon and Fox, 2006; Hawkins, 2011; Menga, 2017). The tenants of the hydro-hegemony analysis theory (see Chapter 1) also go beyond the classical scope, with the introduction of neo-Gramscian grasps of hegemony and hydropolitics.

The focus here coincides in some respects with the proposal made by Turton (2002) but goes beyond it in others. Clearly, regional phenomena cannot be fully understood if local or global elements are left aside. Simultaneously, other dimensions, intersecting territories and states, related to other social aspects of space, such as practices of capital or emancipation, are also relevant. Here, I believe, is where my approach adds to the one proposed by Turton. Social categories of class, race and gender, among others, and relations of property and production should be fundamental to the analysis. Seminal work by Henri Lefebvre (2000) and David Harvey (2001), as well as from other scholars with a radical view on geography and geopolitics, has shown the importance of keeping in mind the interconnections between different scales and spaces. The theoretical approach that I propose (Chapter 1) is multiscalar. As for the empirical topics covered, this study dwells to a large degree on interstate water affairs but also peeks into the water-related grudges and projects mobilised by resistance movements. It should also be mentioned that most of the cases covered in Chapters 2–4 deal with the domestic, regional and global scales in a historical, diachronic perspective, while other equally important aspects are left aside.

All this has to do with the importance that I attribute to writing from a historical vantage point and taking seriously into account the mode of production in which hydropolitcs develops. In both these senses, I draw from the methodological proposal synthesised from Walter Benjamin (1989), Reinhardt Koselleck and others by Enzo Traverso (2012, 17–23), to write history from the point of view of the oppressed, the vanquished. In the long run, this leads to more profound historical knowledge, eventually useful, let us hope, for the agency of subaltern subjects. The importance of taking distance from narrow economistic conceptions of social and political phenomena, while in keeping with a materialist understanding of history, converges with what Michael Löwy (2013) calls Weberian Marxism. Some might find surprising the ways in which I approach the world, Middle Eastern societies, modernity, capitalism and politics. This might have to do with my writing from an anti-Orientalist point of view, drawing from Said (2016) and Achcar (2013), and from Latin America, heeding the call made by Enrique Dussel (2014) to write, in a global postcolonial world, about the South from the South.

The book discusses some axial lines of what I call fluid modernity. Dealing with the entire range of fluid modernity phenomena would require a much greater undertaking, and therefore falls beyond its objectives. It tackles water as a subject of political modernity, which crucially involves not only power relations, understood as complex, multidirectional processes, but also public works and private profits. In fluid modernity, waterworks serve both their stated purposes and the not-so-explicit objective of profit making. Integrating water discourses and infrastructures, *water apparatuses* are produced. They contribute to making populations feel part of the *status quo*, thus strengthening the *governmental reason*. Along international watercourses, some states have sought to mobilise an analogous power relations process over other states in transboundary watercourses to produce *international governmental reasons*. As shown in the following pages, the probability of success of these efforts is far from certain.

To illustrate how these forms of fluid modernity work on the international arena, in this book we focus on water relations between Israel and Arab states and between Turkey, Syria and Iraq. Undoubtedly, numerous examples of international water negotiations, agreements and cooperation, very often alongside coercion, conflict and even instances of war, exist around the globe, but they fall beyond the scope of this text. As for the Middle East, many important hydropolitical events have taken place during the last decades that would have been interesting to include here, but hopefully the cases covered will be enough to illustrate the overall process. Two 21st-century examples worth noting include the building of the Renaissance Dam (Sadd al-Nahda) in Ethiopia, which has put this country at odds with Egypt, or the damming activity carried out by Iran on Tigris tributaries with important consequences on the Iraqi side of the border.

Although separating the international and regional issues from the domestic ones makes sense, the two realms are not sufficiently detached from each other to necessarily justify dealing with them in separate chapters. Hydrology and politics, geography and history come to my aid. The Jordan-Yarmuk River System includes the Eastern slopes of the Mountain Aquifer in the West Bank and the East Bank wadis in Jordan. The Gaza Aquifer is the lower end of the Mountain and Coastal Aquifers. Moreover, these territories and their settlement patterns are historically linked. And so are the politics of the so-called Palestinian-Israeli and Arab-Israeli conflicts, which include the water issues. Therefore, I decided to deal with the water politics that affect Palestinians in connection with hydropolitics among states. Similarly, hydropolitics in the Mesopotamian rivers directly affect Kurds, who inhabit the basin to a very large extent. Not only have Turkey, Syria and Iraq gotten involved in water politics to advance their interests, Kurds have operated in this domain as well. Islamic State in Iraq and Syria (ISIS), which sought to become a state, also worked out its own hydropolitics along the Tigris and Euphrates basins. The book proceeds as follows.

In Chapter 1, water is discussed as a modern subject by grappling with the linkages between large works of infrastructure, particularly waterworks, with the development of capital and modern power. I contend that they play a role in the production of the governmental reason, which is key to the efficient management of populations. Beyond individual states, the more powerful ones also seek to establish a kind of international governmental reason through which they expect weaker states and ruling classes to feel as if they were part of the whole and collaborate with their overall goals. The chapter shows how the New Deal promoted huge regional development schemes such as the Tennessee Valley Authority (TVA), along with other monumental infrastructure works, bringing about full-fledged fluid modernity, which in later decades turned into a paradigm to be replicated internationally. While capitalist interests benefited magnificently, it was also intended to bolster US world political leadership in the longer run.

Chapter 2 deals with the introduction of full-fledged fluid modernity in the Middle East towards the middle of the 20th century. To be sure, an earlier water modernity had been developing in the Ottoman Empire and during the times of European control over a very large part of the region after the First World War. A few decades later, however, once the Second World War was over, the United States deployed extraordinary efforts to establish a new international economic and political order under its leadership in which the region was to play a key geostrategic role on account of its petroleum resources and its location. Water diplomacy and infrastructure financing proposals were deemed instrumental in these efforts. It was an entire international water apparatus in the making.

A geo-historical process, fluid modernity has taken diverse forms in different geographical settings over time. Chapter 3 deals with developments in relation to water in the Middle East from the end of the Suez War of 1956 until the end of the 1980s. Fluid modernity processes in the basins of the region share some characteristics. Each of the two strongest, Western-aligned states in them, Israel and Turkey, followed a mainly coercion-oriented pattern, both vis-à-vis co-riparian states and towards populations living within their borders but considered ethnically or nationally alien, or even non-existent. Through different interventions, including, but not limited to, military action, these states worked to establish their superior position in relation to others in the basins. The chapter shows that weaker states usually sought to fight the coercive version of fluid modernity. Within borders, important sections of the oppressed nations, Palestinian or Kurdish, fought colonisation as well as the water apparatus or many of its effects upon them.

Contemporary Middle East history, neoliberalism and the end of the Cold War overlapped to produce effectual changes on regional politics, giving a new spin to fluid modernity in the region. Chapter 4 traces these evolutions to show the ups and downs of coercion- and hegemony-oriented hydropolitics during the period beginning in 1991. The United States and its regional allies sought to revive the post-Second World War paradigm of turning co-riparian states and proto-states into stakeholders of fluid modernity and its benefits and, together with other mechanisms, to set up an interstate governmental reason. This worked to several extents through what others have called hydrohegemony, implying that conflict was never eliminated, but expressed in different forms. The chapter also shows that, in fluid modernity, diverse organised rebellious movements tend to develop their own hydropolitics.

1 On fluid modernity

"This, gentlemen," said Jeff, "is Columbus River. [If] widened, and deepened, and straightened, and made long enough, it would be one of the finest rivers in the western country."

(An engineer in Mark Twain and Charles Dudley Warner, *The Gilded Age: A Tale of Today*, 1873)

It might be difficult to find a better expression of fledgling fluid modernity than the one depicting the optimism of Jeff Thompson, an engineer in *The Gilded Age*, the novel co-authored by Twain and Dudley. This tributary of a great river could be turned into one of the finest in the country if it only were "widened, deepened, straightened and made long enough". Dominating nature, twisting it at will, turning it into resources have been the pride of capitalism in the last couple of centuries, and water is certainly no exception. The management of things goes hand in hand not only with capital accumulation, but also with the administration of populations, small and large, and their getting involved in the game of getting rich, or simply believing that they could.

This chapter deals with how fluid modernity has come to be and how it has become part of biopolitics, integrated into the development of domestic and international governmental reasons through the production of water apparatuses. It seeks to establish the connections between it and capitalism and how it made a leap in the 20th century with the New Deal and the post-Second World War period. It also retraces some of the main scholarly discussions that have taken place in the last few decades on hydropolitics, particularly those centred on the Middle East to reflect on how the idea of fluid modernity can shed new light on a now old debate.

DOI: 10.4324/9781003356905-2

1.1 A fluid mechanism

It seems quite obvious to understand water in modern society, with all the infrastructure, bureaucracy and trade that it involves, as a matter of technical modernisation. Technical changes have implications so deep for social conviviality that they have turned the fluid into a subject of modernity in a broader, deeper sense. Just two centuries ago, nobody would have imagined that the distribution point in the neighbourhood or even the town well would be gradually phased out and cease being a relevant site for men or women to come together. The later introduction of bathrooms in private homes reduced the importance of public baths and the forms of socialisation associated with them. More recently, even the systematic act of offering water to your neighbour with its various meaningful implications has lost ground to the individuation required by the almost universal sale of plastic water bottles. A small part of an ever-growing context of generalised market relations taking hold of societies worldwide, the disposable water bottle business encourages people to cut themselves from one another. The difference between having water offered by often unknown people and buying it reminds me of the difference between asking someone to make a photo of you or making a selfie with the resulting withering of social interactions even in such minute forms. The broader articulation of modernity covers a very large range of aspects in the realm of ideas, conducts and knowledge, and, to put it in the words of Saurabh Dube (2017, 76), in processes "of empire and colony, race and genocide, resurgent faiths and reified traditions, disciplinary regimes and subaltern subjects, and the seductions of the state and enchantments of the modern".

Water has become a subject of modernity in other relevant ways as well. Modern decision makers, industrialists, scientists, engineers, thinkers, human beings in general, have sought to control nature and all things natural in the last few centuries like never before. As Horkheimer and Adorno (2002) put it,

> Myth becomes enlightenment and nature mere objectivity. Human beings purchase the increase in their power with estrangement from that over which it is exerted. Enlightenment stands in the same relationship to things as the dictator to human beings. He knows them in the extent that he can manipulate them.

As Pfaffenberger (1988) explains—following Marx, but also MacKenzie and Wajcman—technology is actually social relations, nature humanised, and its impact on society is the impact of a certain kind of social behaviour. In relation to water, rivers are dammed, drills seek the liquid hundreds of meters deep, weather modification offices use cannons and planes to produce or prevent rainfall at will, not to mention the growing and overarching implications that carbon capitalism, *id est*, industrial capitalism, has had on world climate and therefore precipitation patterns. In the process, natural habitats have been radically altered, changing the conditions for life and reducing biodiversity. Nature is no more, having been appropriated, turned into mere resources waiting to be exploited (Smith, 2008; Selby, 2003) for the modern production of goods and services that require huge amounts of water worldwide. Humans have come to consider water itself as unruly (Gibbs, 2010; Hawkins, 2011). Water requirements under present modes of production and consumption go far beyond daily household needs, which explains scarcity, even in regions not usually considered arid, and a generalised need to expand water availability. Agriculture and livestock breeding take the largest part, but industry, before accounting for the production of the raw materials it requires, takes a considerable percentage as well, while city and household uses often come third.[1] Thus, the capitalist urge to always make and accumulate more profits gets bound to the modern desire to subject nature, turning it into "natural resources", including water.

In tandem, the subject of water has become hydropolitics in several forms, finding its way into governmentality alongside other better studied apparatuses, entangled with them, having quite impressive implications in the production of power and politics within the modern nation-state and in the international state order. Michel Foucault (1971, 1979) discussed how the linkages between a complex array of discursive and material elements produce a power system that plays a key role in the *governmental reason*, which binds state and subjects in rather subtle ways through the administration of life, as a shepherd who cares for his sheep. These mechanisms are different from what Antonio Gramsci (1971) described as hegemony, the dialectical combination of coercion and consensus, through which the ruling classes strive to bring subaltern subjects in as stakeholders in the exercise of power and the preservation of the *status quo*. The governmental reason is the product of biopolitics, the idea that the state cares for the life of the populations it administers, which renders power not only cheaper to operate, but much more efficient than policing, built on the basis of several interconnected and often overlapping apparatuses, such as the security apparatus. In this book, I suggest that water, with its growing practical and symbolic importance, and the intricate technologies involved in making it readily available, has become a *water apparatus*.

The governmental reason insists less on clear-cut interests, which differ throughout society, than on the well-being of all and comprehensive ideas and practices. The nation, for example, is an abstract but engaging concept that crosses through class, gender, sect, race, region, extended family and other meaningful groups, and thereby includes most or at least many subaltern subjects, even though they have interests of their own. The state, at least under "normal circumstances", cares for the life of its population, seeks to sustain livelihoods, feeds the hungry, quenches the thirsty, cares for the ill and makes jobs available for the needy, while fostering big and profitable business for the wealthy. How could anyone oppose the profit-making expansion of waterworks when many go hungry or lack steady jobs in town and country, quite notably, though not exclusively, in the Global South? After all, governmentality (the governmental reason) results from biopolitics, the management of life (and death, as argued further on) of real people and other living beings within the state or even across borders.

Water stands among many other subjects, such as technology, territory, energy, as a key building block of the state, of the nation. Writing about the history of the uses of water in 20th-century Mexico, Luis Aboites (1998) titled his book "The Water of the Nation". Dams were planned as fabulous structures meant to represent the grandeur and power of the state (Steinberg, 1993; Pritchard, 2011; Domínguez, 2019). Scholars dealing with international rivers engage in what has been called "methodological nationalism" (Kauffer, 2018; Wheeler and Hussein, 2021). Water has been broadly utilised around the world to legitimise the state and strengthen the idea of the nation, domestically and even abroad (Allouche, 2020). For example, as will become apparent in Chapter 4, Turkish officials have gone as far as claiming that water captured in their territory is Turkish, even if it feeds a cross-border river system like the Tigris-Euphrates. In 1990, Turkish President Turgut Özal and Prime Minister Süleyman Demirel made the claim in separate instances (Chalabi and Majzoub, 1995, 211) and even argued that water flowing through their territory is the property of their nation, just like Arab oil is Arab, which entitles them to trade it in similar mercantile terms. The governmental reason uses of such nationalist conceptions of water and, we should add, of dams are a crucial part of fluid modernity.

Discourses apart, social realities and interests do exist, even in relation to water, although they may get concealed behind the rationale governing the fluid in modern societies, let alone overarching entities or compounds of countries neighbouring each other. For many subaltern subjects, water development seems compelling because it allows them to satisfy vital needs and get jobs, in agriculture, industry, services or even informal sectors, from building a dam to tilling irrigated lands, working in water bottling companies or collecting plastic bottles for recycling. For proprietors, although feeding the many surely makes sense, they most immediately appreciate having the cash register ring with water infrastructure projects and their derivatives in finance, construction, manufacturing, agribusiness, commerce, tourism, recycling or any other related industry.

The governmental reason, with its apparatuses, however, is not all-powerful, which leads the sovereign power of the state to include, within the biopolitical administration of life, its contrary, i.e., exclusion and the negation of life, thanatopolitics (Agamben, 1998). Times of crisis come to be, and "states of exception" are declared, where a deadly state violence is unleashed (Agamben, 2005), even by states where conflict is usually regulated (Traverso, 2012, 206–209). Ever more often, the state of exception gets "normalised" and becomes the rule, permanent, from the point of view of the oppressed (Benjamin, 1989). This state of exception is sometimes confined to specific—not only long lasting, but often large—spaces that may get called something indicating their "exceptional character", such as "special" (Herrera Santana, 2020, 25–26) or "interim".

Subaltern subjects often see through power networks, particularly when they are altogether left out of the nation itself, which is commonly constructed on difference and exclusion, and they get excluded from life-caring biopower, becoming the target of discrimination, repression and thanatopolitics. In such situations, people come to oppose the governmental reason in passive or active resistance, and eventually go all the way to produce their own counter-hegemonic frames or even societal alternatives. The differentiation in social realities and interests produces numerous vertical and horizontal contradictions in national, social, economic and political arenas, which may lead to subjection, negotiation, rebellion.

Thus, not all subaltern subjects will accept the nationalist, hegemonic framing of water. In a more pragmatic key, they may oppose the building of a reservoir bound to displace many, drown extensive surfaces of often the best agricultural lands, wipe out habitats, obliterate meaningful spaces, segment their geography or favour certain other people—often richer, more connected or with better claims to national appurtenance—in, for example, acquiring the lands that will benefit the most from the resulting changes in water distribution or enjoy hydropower hundreds of kilometres away. In spite of ideological discourses surrounding water and reservoirs, numerous examples of social struggles around them exist in Asia, Africa and Latin America (see, among many others, Gómez *et al.*, 2014; Marston and Hoeur, 2016).

Within individual states, the governmental reason embedded in fluid modernity takes diverse forms. In previous paragraphs, I have tried to reflect on the ways in which the water apparatus works in general. The cases brought up in this book, centred in the Middle East, illustrate some of its features when operating within the borders of a particular state. Considering the water relations between Israel and the Palestinians, and Turkey and the Kurds shows how the biopolitics of the water apparatus affects groups that the governmental reason designates as alien, as causing a state of emergency. It becomes apparent that states integrate water into nationalist narratives and develop large waterworks, such as the Israeli National Water Carrier or the Turkish South East Anatolia Project (GAP), to strengthen a water apparatus that tightens population-state bonds among those considered part of the nation while excluding the *other* from its benefits, in these cases Palestinians and Kurds. At the end of this fragment I think it should read: "their territories or their societies" (in plural) (Soleimani and Mohammadpour, 2022). This of course happens also in other regions, with other peoples, around the world (see, for example, Wilson *et al.*, 2021). Conversely, resistance movements have integrated the question of water into their lists of grievances, into their strategies of resistance and rebellion, and whenever possible into practices of liberation.

For geo-historical reasons, many watercourses constitute political borders or flow across them, and efforts to control their resources usually end up affecting water availability or quality for inhabitants of other countries within basins. If water constitutes a relevant element in the within-borders power apparatus and the economy, control over water resources by one state in an international basin may weaken control by another, thereby undermining the domestic governmental reason, economy and interests of the latter and of its ruling classes. From these situations, interstate power struggles develop, which include conflicts, resistance, negotiations and even cooperation.

If waterworks and in general water politics are efficient elements of the domestic power system, they are often put at the service of complex power mechanisms at the regional or even the world scale. An effort is made to replicate at a supra-state level the mechanisms of governmentality that work so well in the domestic domain. Foucault (2008, 55–56) mentions that Europe managed to produce a continental governmental reason by developing a non-zero-sum game based on an "increasingly extending [world] market". Although often clumsily, not even mostly under non-zero-sum-game settings, water apparatuses have become part of international governmental reasons. The different chapters of this book illustrate this process in frameworks of conflict and cooperation, efforts at domination by some states and active resistance by others and practices of hegemony, combining force and consensus. Regional water regimes and epistemic communities of water scientists are typical mechanisms of a successful—or rather successful—international water apparatus (for illustration, see the contrasting approaches to these phenomena by Rodríguez Echavarría, 2018; Kibaroğlu, 2002).

It should be mentioned that scales are seldom so neatly differentiated into clear-cut realms as the international and the domestic. As seen in Chapter 4, Israel manages water for itself and to an extent for the Palestinians, many of whom live, since the implementation of the Oslo Agreements, under a Palestinian Authority which is autonomous only to a certain degree, even in relation to water. It is quite unclear whether we should consider this a case of domestic or international fluid modernity, and might actually be both at the same time and something else, as we deal here with a colonial settler state in postcoloniality. The same applies to when Turkey severely slashes the flow of Euphrates water to affect the Kurds of north-east Syria. It seeks to disrupt the Rojava autonomous self-rule experience in order to curb domestic challenges from Bakur Kurds, i.e., those living within the geopolitical borders of the Republic of Turkey.[2] These are instances of overlapping domestic and international water apparatuses.

1.2 Fluid modernity and capitalism

Fluid modernity is a historical process in which full-fledged fluid modernity in the era of large-scale development of water infrastructure represents its apex, at least so far. In capitalist times, large-scale water management and the construction of waterworks are not only about the obvious and less obvious uses of water, but also about making profits. Water for husbandry, industry, urban and household uses is of course important, particularly in times of biopolitics in which consumption patterns under capitalism and populations have experienced unprecedented growth. Where average people think of use values and social needs, fluid modernity is very much about exchange value, profits, although also about power and culture. The construction industry soars with contracts whenever a new dam is built. During the 1990s, dam building around the world was an industry worth between $32 and $46 billion dollars per year, or a sum total of approximately $2 trillion during the 20th century (McCully, 2001, xxvii). If the reservoir is part of a more ambitious development project, as is often the case in full-fledged fluid modernity, the number of contracts multiplies. Along with waterworks, often come roads, power grids, canals, new towns and so on. Another beneficiary is the financial sector, as such projects require colossal loans, loan guarantees, insurance policies and other investment-banking services.

Although humans have used water for irrigation for around 9 millennia and to power mills for 2000 years (McNeill, 2000), during the last few centuries water and water infrastructure have taken on a new dimension in the economy and in governance. The great empires of the past, based on agriculture and husbandry, harnessed water whenever possible through dams and canals to increase their wealth and power. Construction, however, was an investment rather than a profit-making industry itself. During the last few centuries, the use of water has multiplied in gross and relative figures. McNeill (2000) gives estimates of global freshwater use from 1700 to 2000, which show that yearly gross water consumption grew from 110 km^3 in 1700 to 580 in 1900 and 5190 in 2000. Withdrawals per capita more than doubled during the three centuries from 1700 to 1900, and again more than doubled from 1900 to 2000. The proportion of the fluid that was being used for agriculture roughly remained unchanged between 1700 and 1900 but went down from the previous 90% to 83% in 1950 and to 64% in 2000, which implies an inversely proportional increase in industrial, urban and household uses. While in 1900 only one million Americans were connected to sewer systems, by the 1970s the figure had grown to 170 million (Barnet, 1980).

Already in early modern France, in the late 16th century, King Henry IV used water as a means to legitimate his power among Catholic Parisians. Himself a Huguenot who had to convert to Catholicism, he came to the throne after religious wars had been ravaging the country and Paris itself. Parisian Catholics only accepted him half-heartedly. The King had the Samaritaine Pump and the Rugis Aqueduc, or Aqueduc d'Arceuil, built to improve water availability and distribution in the city. The ability to expand the city and improve the quality of life of its dwellers had been limited for lack of water. What is crucial for our discussion, however, is that the waterworks allowed Henry IV to show leadership and better ground his legitimacy (Mukerji, 2017, 30–36).

Although, as may be clear by now, this book focuses on water for non-navigational uses, it should be noted that fluid modernity is not unrelated to the building of other types of infrastructure, including of course canals for the opening up of navigation routes, aiming to annihilate space with time, to use the expression coined by Karl Marx (cited by Harvey, 2001), in the process of capitalist accumulation. An early modern instance concerned the construction starting in 1666, of the *Canal du Midi*, linking the Atlantic Ocean to the Mediterranean Sea. Jean-Baptiste Colbert, Controller-General of Finances of Louis XIV, directed important resources to build infrastructure in the second half of the 17th century, which would eventually lead to the establishment of the Corps of Bridges and Roads. Chandra Mukerji (2009) shows how this impressive piece of infrastructure contributed to produce power and knowledge. More crucially, perhaps, it helped build the impersonal power of the state, still under the *Ancien Régime*, by mobilising different sections of society in southwestern France regardless of their pre-existing social bonds, in a region where people still resented previous religious wars. Worldwide, many other later canals, together with railroads, would become conspicuous subjects of modernity, Empire and Nation, including of course the ones in Suez and Panama.

Infrastructure as technology, as previously hinted, is not simply a means to a material end, charged with quite complex connections not only to the economy, but to individuals, societies and politics—to social space. Through infrastructure, a certain order is given to space with the aim of increasing profits, reducing costs for capital accumulation. Water structures are outstanding mechanisms that produce social space usually for capital while destroying previously existing social spaces. Interventions by the state or companies through fixed elements such as reservoirs have effects on many sorts of flow. Flooding valleys to accumulate water in artificial lakes hampers the movement of people and animals, for example, and generates new circulations—of water, people, goods, capital—where and when those in control of the structure choose. In the process, large sectors, particularly the most vulnerable, often get dispossessed of spaces that used to be common to all.

Starting from a basic definition of infrastructure—meditated and dynamic forms that produce and transform socio-technical relations, generate effects and structure social relations—Penelope Harvey *et al.* (2017) point to its open-ended relational capacities to underscore the impossibility of inferring how people apprehend infrastructures as relevant to them. In sum, these authors agree with others that infrastructure is part of society, politics and economics.

Infrastructures, including reservoirs and other waterworks, have proven key to capitalist development in numerous forms. Speaking of an "infrastructural power", Herrera Santana (2019) shows how infrastructure takes a strong political and even geopolitical character by allowing states and investors not only to connect the spaces that capitalism fragments, but also to ensure capitalist penetration and territorial appropriation of regions of high strategic value. Infrastructures also promise "modernity, development, progress, and freedom" (Appel *et al.*, 2018, 3). Anand *et al.* (2018), following Joyce (2003), explain that infrastructure became a key technology of government, modelling relations between state, society and corporations, guaranteeing the liberties of some and the subjection of others. The same goes, I would add, for waterworks of all sorts; not only are they produced by state, business and society or objected to by many or few, but they also have predictable and unpredictable implications in different domains, particularly in the governmental reason, as I have sought to argue.

The United States, entering fluid modernity early on with the building of dams and waterways, became the core of full-fledged fluid modernity during the second third of the 20th century. On average, one reservoir has been inaugurated there every year since 1776, but building dams, as well as other infrastructure, became key to the New Deal and to Keynesian economics in general since the 1930s. Huge government budgets went to construction projects that boosted the economy after the Great Depression. New Dealers came to realise that public works not only allowed people to get jobs, but brought many into the political fold, contributing to the establishment of the basis for US "democracy and the American way of life" (Klein, 1999). Between 1933 and 1939, two of every three dollars in the monumental federal emergency funds went to public works, paying for programmes such as the Boulder (Hoover) Dam or the Tennessee Valley Authority (TVA), which amounted to what has been called a "public works" revolution that helped legitimise the new role of the state in managing the US economy and boost state-led economic development by relying on private contractors (Smith, 2009). The very title of the influential book by David Lilienthal (1953), *TVA: Democracy on the March*, tells a lot about the assumptions of the operation.

While fluid modernity made a qualitative leap during the New Deal years and afterwards to become a successfully bolstered governmental economic, social and cultural phenomenon in the United States, after the Second World War it was turned into a model to conquer the hearts and minds of people and leaders around the planet. New Deal public works went global after the war with enormous infrastructure programmes, which included the building of dams inspired by the TVA. The geopolitical setup of the Cold War—in which countries had little alternative but to choose between following the United States or the Soviet Union—implied keeping the military industry running and affirming spaces of leadership globally. This had wide implications in organising the world in military, economic and political terms. While the North Atlantic Treaty

Organization (NATO) was to affirm US military hegemony in Europe, the Bretton Woods organisations, the International Monetary Fund (IMF) and the World Bank, were to establish the ascendancy of the US dollar and economy. US governments and companies have always had a strong influence over the World Bank (Toussaint, 2022, 121–146). The International Bank for Reconstruction and Development (IBRD), a key institution of the World Bank system, went on a lending spree for the reconstruction of Europe parallel to the Marshall Plan. In his 1949 inaugural speech, US President Harry Truman announced a major foreign policy objective to be added to promoting the United Nations, the Marshall Plan and NATO: to launch a bold new programme to employ US know-how and resources to aid "underdeveloped" nations (Smith, 2009, 248–250). US historian and White House adviser Arthur M. Schlesinger Jr. stated it candidly: the "Tennessee Valley Authority is a weapon which, if properly employed, might outbid all the social ruthlessness of the Communists for support of the people of Asia" (cited by Smith, 2009, 250).

The United States invested enormous efforts after the Second World War in fluid modernity schemes. Turning the TVA into a global operation was part of a number of initiatives aimed at establishing an international governmental reason to make US hegemony a more or less subtle, self-reproducing mechanism. Already in 1944, US diplomacy had applied the water apparatus in international relations with Mexico, when the two countries signed a relatively benign bilateral water agreement in spite of the power asymmetry between them (Samaniego, 2006).[3] Although the IBRD allocated its first loans to the reconstruction of Europe, it soon extended them for development projects outside the continent, with a good proportion going for reservoirs and other water infrastructure. Before the 1940s came to an end, the Bank had financed water projects in Chile, Mexico and Brazil. Countries in Asia soon followed: Japan in the late 1940s with the adoption of a TVA-like development mentality (Dinmore, 2013); India with the Damodar Act in 1948, which provided for the Damodar Valley Corporation (Hamilton, 1969); Afghanistan with the 1952 Helmand Valley Authority, which evoked ideas of development and modernity (Cullather, 2002); Indochina with the 1954 establishment and 1957 amplification of the Mekong Committee (Campbell, 2016). Something along the same lines was proposed for the management of the Indus River by India and Pakistan when negotiations for the Indus Water Treaty started in the 1950s, which eventually led to the adoption of the Indus Basin Plan in Pakistan. As Akhter (2015) rightly observes, the Indus Water Treaty negotiations, with World Bank intervention, show the works of "inter-scalar cultural and political economic processes" in times of "hydropolitical Cold War". The mechanism was extended to other continents, including Africa. In 1967, the US Bureau of Reclamation proposed to establish in Tanzania a National Water Resource Council to dam the Rufiji River (Hoag, 2006).

In the post-war era, Washington bureaucrats operated on such water apparatuses to achieve very concrete geopolitical/hydropolitical goals. Ambitious water development plans were also promoted in the Middle East. As will be seen in Chapter 2, from the beginning of the Cold War, the US State Department formulated a policy proposal to use funds for water infrastructure projects to lure the newly independent Arab countries into US hegemony and into recognising Israel as a legitimate state in the region. In the early 1950s, the World Bank offered funding to Egypt for a huge dam on the Nile at Aswan, to Syria to drain the Ghab Swamps and develop them for agriculture and to establish a comprehensive development plan around a large dam on the Euphrates (Salman, 2009). An important Arab-Israeli negotiation scheme was proposed around the Jordan basin. All this occurred as the United States and its allies were seeking to establish a military mechanism for the Middle East analogous to NATO.

Fascinating in itself, not to mention being profitable for large construction-industry corporations, fluid modernity captured the imagination of politicians, engineers, business people and citizens in multiple ways. During the following decades, usually with enticing international funding available, countries in the Middle East as elsewhere continued developing water infrastructure in intra- and trans-boundary rivers with diverse hydropolitical consequences. During this period, the United States worked on the basis of the new mindset hoping to extend its governmentality over the entire region (Chapter 2). Once these efforts failed, a state of exception was declared in the region, and aid was given to states addicted to its governmental reason while excluding the rebellious ones. This also reflected in the stronger states in the region developing coercive politics in general, and in relation to water as well, as the hydropolitics of Israel, Turkey (Chapter 3) and Egypt show.

As neoliberalism took hold of decision makers around the Capitalist world and the Cold War came to an end, hydropolitics took a new turn. As the neoclassical doctrine watered down the economic role of the state, the pace of building monumental water projects receded, and private water utilities were granted ownership, or at least concessions, over entire water networks. Nonetheless, many reservoirs have been built during these decades, usually with substantial state aid, but in which private companies have taken a more relevant role in construction and management of the infrastructure works. In this context, as will be seen in Chapter 4, states have continued to carry out hydropolitics although often with a more variable political spin than during the previous decades, particularly in transboundary basins.[4]

1.3 The Middle East hydropolitics debate

This book discusses water politics in terms of fluid modernity, biopolitics, governmentality and the establishment of water apparatuses. Usually, however, scholars have discussed hydropolitics, particularly when dealing with the Middle East, in terms of the more traditional schools of International Relations theory, although sometimes with a critical twist. This section recapitulates some of the core debates that have taken place around water in the region. (See the location of the rivers of the Middle East discussed in this book in Map 1.1.)

It is actually a *cliché* to say that the Middle East suffers from water scarcity. In part, this idea comes from Western imaginations of exotic Arabian deserts and in part from ideological conceptions of the Near East constructed with quite concrete political objectives. For instance, Alatout (2008) shows how Israeli ideologues passed from a discourse of water abundance to one of scarcity in order to justify a turn of the state from agricultural to industrial and urban development. Nonetheless, analysts have observed that by the mid-1990s, almost all Arab states and Israel already were consuming over 40% of available renewable resources (Ecosoc, 1997; Seckler *et al.*, 1998; Allan, 2001). Many inhabitants in the area get along with small volumes. Of course, mentioning the overall gravity of the situation can lead us to overlook key sub-regional differences in terms of precipitation, superficial and underground watercourses, unconventional water development technologies, the relative importance of agriculture for jobs and subsistence, and financial capacity to improve water management or import "virtual water", i.e., goods that require water for their production instead of growing or manufacturing them domestically.[5]

The water conflict in the Jordan-Yarmuk and Mountain Aquifer basins between Israel and Lebanon, Syria, Jordan and the Palestinians has been minutely researched. The conflict over the Nile, and that between Turkey, Syria and Iraq over the Tigris and Euphrates Rivers have also commanded many studies. Much of the theory on water wars, negotiations, hydropolitics and hydro-hegemony has emanated from these watercourses. The complexity of these conflicts stems from several factors, including the fact that in parts of the area more water is consumed every year than what gets renewed; the involved states have lived in a permanent state of war for decades; military clashes have

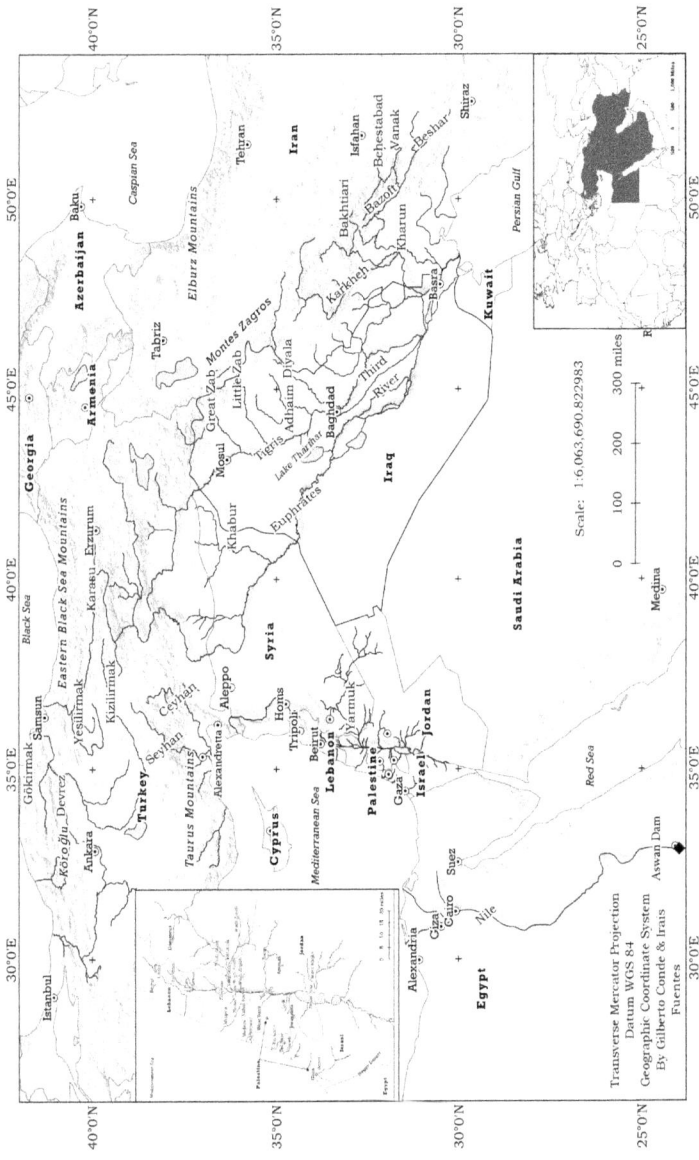

Map 1.1 Tigris, Euphrates, Jordan and Asi/Orontes Rivers. Map by the author and Iraís Fuentes.

already taken place in which water has been a strategic or tactic aim, despite numerous rounds of negotiations and even cooperation over the fluid. The region has been considered strategic by world powers, as several US presidential doctrines show.

Authors have discussed whether water scarcity constitutes a kind of imperative that pushes some countries, such as Israel or Iraq, into waging wars to secure access to the fluid or avoiding peace for similar reasons. Writing in the times of the Madrid and Oslo negotiations processes and their immediate aftermath, an imperative-for-negotiation, liberal-institutional group argued that other criteria than water have always had priority in war-making and that, on the contrary, water was so important that it always pushed parties to negotiate (Wolf, 1995, 2000; Biswas *et al.*, 1997; Dolatyar and Gray, 1999; Hof, 2000; Kay and Mitchell, 2000; Kliot, 2000; Lonergan, 2000). Boutros Boutros Ghali in the mid-1980s, before he became Secretary General of the United Nations, asserted that the wars of the future in the Middle East would be waged for water (cited by Chesnot, 1993; Starr, 1995). In line with this assessment, an imperative-for-war, realist group sustained that at least some of the fighting that has taken place in the region had already been carried out due to water needs and that it has led countries such as Israel to avoid relinquishing water-sensitive territories (Bulloch and Darwish, 1993; Beaumont, 2000; Rowley, 2000; Klare, 2001; Ward, 2002). In the debate, another group of realist authors not only recognised that wars can be and have been waged over water but also asserted that control of the fluid can allow a state to extend its power over others (Naff and Matson, 1984; Lowi, 1995; Gleick, 1992, 2000).

Empirical data seems to confirm that water has been a goal of both peace and war in numerous instances in rivers like the Jordan-Yarmuk, although it certainly has not been their only aim, nor even the main one. As discussed throughout this book, it would seem that water and related infrastructure projects have been both a cause and an excuse for fighting in the 1950s, the 1960s, the 1968–1970 period and the 1980s. It helped entice peace negotiations in the 1990s, was used as an argument to avoid it in 2000 and again became a target of military operations in several instances thereafter.

Drawing from Gramscian understandings of power, the London Water Study Group has theorised about hydro-hegemony, discussing the complex array of relations over water, mainly among states. They tend to rule out that wars aim at securing water and insist more on the different mechanisms employed by the more powerful party on a watercourse that usually enable it to push its water-related decisions on co-riparian states through a combination of conflict and negotiation

(Zeitoun and Mirumachi, 2008; Zeitoun *et al.*, 2011, 2017). They argue that the central questions do not revolve around the existence of water conflict, but around the intensity with which it manifests itself and how the most powerful country in a basin establishes hydro-hegemony over its neighbours (see, for example, Zeitoun and Warner, 2006; Daoudy, 2008; Warner, 2010; Zeitoun, 2011; Warner *et al.*, 2013).

The water aspects of these disputes are structurally linked to other, non-water issues, such as overall power relations, hegemony and domination involving riparian states and people and often also extra-riparian states (Warner, 2010). Warner *et al.* (2013) explain that many basins present a mix of cooperation and conflict framed within a series of non-violent manifestations of power aimed at engaging other actors through "soft power".

During the 1990s, water was an outstanding point in talks between Arabs and Israelis in the Madrid Process, the Oslo deals, the Jordanian-Israeli Peace Treaty and Syrian-Israeli peace talks. These dealings, as Mark Zeitoun (2011) has shown, were water conflict through other means and established in writing the ascendancy of Israel, the most powerful party in the watershed. Thus, negotiation and cooperation between states over water issues, far from excluding hydro-hegemonic relations, are the way to enthrone them effectively (Warner *et al.*, 2013). Soft power mechanisms tend to work better, underscoring the consensus part of the hegemony equation. When a state, seeking to exploit its strengths, tries to impose outright its decisions on other states, they opt for hard power. In these cases, the weaker countries often fight back and seek to develop what we could also call counter-hegemonic measures. Negotiations may include *token proposals*, which give the appearance of a willingness to concede although only provisional agreements are granted, thereby holding out the threat of a return to more aggressive, hydro-coercive policies. Let us insist, final agreements tend to codify iniquitous relationships.

To summarise, war or even open coercion is not the principal means a state uses to impose its will on others; quite the contrary. War is the exception that confirms the rule of how the international system works. Negotiation and cooperation—usually without cancelling conflict—conceal hegemony, through which the stronger seek to establish a certain relationship with the weaker, allowing the latter to obtain some relative gains from the ensuing situation while keeping most benefits. Rather than confrontation, weaker states usually prefer agreements that give them some benefits which simultaneously allow their leaders to save face with their population as having served well the nation. But when the stronger insist on coercion and domination, the weaker can be resourceful and utilise several mechanisms to produce better results, albeit with risks, costs and time. All this applies to water relations as well.

Jan Selby, another serious scholar on water in the region also ascribing to Gramscian critical theory, has discussed the role of states and society in water politics. Selby (2003, 2005, 2007) contends that the real water conflict in the Middle East opposes not states among themselves, since for them water has only a limited value, but states *versus* populations, the ones who really suffer from water scarcity. Selby (2003) and Zeitoun (2011) agree on an important theoretical and methodological point, namely that water conflicts cannot be understood in isolation from their overall social and political reality.

It should be noted that although Gramsci (2000) developed his thinking on hegemony in relation to the ruling and the subaltern subjects within states, he explains that it also extends to relations among states, even though he focused less on this. Nonetheless, it should be noticed that, as Ives and Short (2013) have shown, Gramsci thought of political phenomena on the domestic, state scale in a dialectical interaction with the international one. This should have implications for how hydro-hegemony should be understood. In any case, the classes which exert their hegemony shed their influence over as many sections of society as possible to consolidate their ascendancy. The model, which usually works well in the domestic arena, has been replicated in international relations. Powerful states seek to include not-so-powerful or outright weak ones through mechanisms that include the distribution of benefits without actually forgoing coercion. While the latter is important, the former is crucial and much more effective in maintaining hegemony, both domestically as among states.

The codification of international water law for non-navigational uses came about with great pains in the second half of the 20th century and has somehow consecrated, I would argue, the fluid modernity mechanisms of the international governmental reason. During the 1990s, while many countries were at loggerheads with each other in relation to water, the UN Legal Committee, which was discussing the draft Convention on the Law of the Non-Navigational Uses of International Watercourses, became yet another arena. The UN General Assembly finally adopted the Convention in 1997, against the votes of Turkey, China and Burundi. The document only became International Treaty Law in 2014 when it was finally ratified by a sufficient number of states. The old nationalist principles of water law that stand at opposite ends, absolute sovereignty and absolute territorial integrity, have cancelled each other out to produce a treaty law that seeks to promote negotiation (McCaffrey, 2001), which tends to favour the more powerful states.

Quite unsurprisingly, as Daoudy (2008, 89–102) and Woodhouse and Zeitoun (2008, 103–119) forecasted, its coming into force has failed to free states from power relations around water.

1.4 Conclusions

In previous publications, I have studied international relations over water from a hydro-hegemony analysis perspective, which clearly has proven fruitful. In this book, however, I decided to reflect on the same issues under a different light. In modern capitalist societies, water and water infrastructure have been increasingly produced not only for profits but by and for the governmental reason, particularly after the Second World War, in radically novel forms. The production of water through intensive human/technical intervention has been fully incorporated into biopower and the governmental reason. People have come to understand the fluid, its fittings and the entire water apparatus as a natural, essential means to everyday life, as the way things simply are. This has penetrated people and society so deeply that water and the means of water production have become part of our very existence, and that of the nation and the state. As the sense of scarcity increases, water, traditionally a common resource, has also been captured as a commodity by private utilities companies.

The development of the water apparatus, constitutive of the governmental reason and therefore of biopolitics, tends to create a social consensus in favour of national control over the liquid. Thus perceived, water seems to justify, in the eyes of social subjects, strong state action for its management and defence. Those in control can easily justify domestic and foreign policies framed in terms of water needs, considered an absolute biopolitical necessity. The fluid is a matter/subject that changes through space and time, according to how subjects produce it in material and symbolic ways. Technological interventions in rivers and aquifers have significant consequences for within- and cross-border populations, not to mention ecosystems. This is especially true under conditions of aridity or scarcity, or when many jobs and profits are related to infrastructure and development projects, to construction, irrigation or hydropower generation.

Notes

1 There are important exceptions to this pattern, which has been changing during the last half century. Two such cases are Israel and Jordan, where household uses take up more water than industry (Zeitoun, 2011).

2 Kurds designate the territories of Kurdistan comprised within Turkey, Iraq, Iran and Syria as Bakur, Bashur, Rojhelat and Rojava, respectively. In their language, these names correspond to the four cardinal points, north, south, east and west of Kurdistan.

3 The deal benefited the United States more and Mexico less than Samaniego (2006) seems to admit, but he correctly argues that even these relatively beneficial terms for Mexico would have been more difficult to achieve in different circumstances.

4 See the stimulating discussion on infrastructure, neoliberalism and revolution in Anand *et al.* (2018), particularly the chapter by Dominic Boyer (2018).

5 Tony Allan (2001) explains that importing goods is equivalent to bringing "virtual water" from afar, saving the water that a country would require to produce them locally.

2 Making fluid modernity in the Middle East

While fluid modernity made headway in the Middle East during the first half of the 20th century, full-fledged fluid modernity was only established during the 1950s. As explained in Chapter 1, the United States produced and tested a water apparatus domestically through New Deal infrastructural programmes such as the Tennessee Valley Authority during the 1930s that proved instrumental in developing the governmental reason and sought to expand it to the international arena after the Second World War. A new dimension was added, as the idea was to make the water apparatus work not only in domestic contexts, to bring citizens into the fold, but also in interstate settings, to bring states to accept the US hegemony that was being established during the period. As it hopefully became clear in Chapter 1, fluid modernity of course was not, is not, only about the development of governmentality, from above and below, but also about making profits. Water, dams and hydro-infrastructure in general have come to play a role in biopolitics, the administration of life, in the domestic and international scale.

The history of fluid modernity has been a history of complex transitions related to the social, cultural changes of modernity in general and to the political and economic transformations of capitalism. The empirical examples used in this book come from a region of the Middle East that was part of the Ottoman Empire until the end of the First World War. These countries have a somewhat common fluid modernity heritage of their own, but one that does not entirely set them apart from other world regions, which have gone through relatively similar, interconnected processes. As part of a series of modernising efforts, the Ottoman Empire introduced a land reform in the second half of the 19th century that led to a radical transformation in land tenure and property. The Empire invested in building water infrastructure in lower Mesopotamia early in the 20th century. However, its early attempts at developing fluid modernity failed to go very far, as the

DOI: 10.4324/9781003356905-3

Empire got dismembered and eventually crumbled after its defeat in the First World War.

Water infrastructure has a longer history in the Middle East, which might not come as a real surprise, given that humans seemingly first began tilling land and watering crops precisely here several millennia ago. Since then, water has been used for agriculture in the watersheds of the Mesopotamia and the Nile Valley, as well as around smaller watercourses such as the Jordan and the Asi/Orontes river basins. Large centres of civilisation have developed around these sources of water since then. Some of these areas, Egypt in particular, even became known as the breadbasket of the Roman Empire.

However, fluid modernity is a more recent phenomenon, as we have tried to explain in the previous chapter. In early and not-so-early modern times, Middle Eastern governments strove to use water to improve soil quality, reduce salinity and increase agricultural yields. The Ottoman Empire during the 19th century, under the rule of Abdulhamid II, introduced agrarian reform and private landownership, and built dams to protect lower Mesopotamia from floods. In Egypt, the British rulers sought to bolster agricultural output, as Mohammed Ali had done before them, with updated technological means. Towards the end of the century, they had a dam built on the Nile. With little more than nominal independence, the Egyptian monarchy over Egypt and Sudan signed an agreement with fellow Nile riparian countries in the 1920s to guarantee the continuous flow of the fluid in the future. The cotton-producing place given to Egypt in the international division of labour required huge amounts of water.

As is well known, the domains of the Empire were partitioned into several states after the First World War and were placed under the more or less direct control of Britain and France—the European victors of the First World War—under the League of Nations mandate system. These rulers took the new states through parallel courses in many respects, including in relation to water resources and infrastructure. Fluid modernity went a step further than what the region had experienced until then. International relations around water developed in the process of partitioning these territories and making them suitable for economic development.

The couple of decades following the Second World War witnessed the difficult birth of the postcolonial order marked by the accession to independence by the colonial states in the region and elsewhere, bringing changes in the interactions among them and between them and world powers. The newly independent states sought to muster their power and resources, including water, to take on their future. The United States, then the new leader of what came to be the Western Bloc, together with the old mandatory metropolis, especially Britain, sought to model the coming era through innovative power techniques, which included those of the water apparatus.

Fluid modernity experienced an important leap on the world scale, propelled by Keynesian economics and lending for large infrastructural works. As seen, the United States played an important role in promoting the drive for dam building in the world. Sections 2.1 and 2.2 explore how fluid modernity evolved during the first half of the century following the economic and biopolitical concerns of the colonial projects in Palestine, and in Syria and Iraq. Sections 2.3–2.5 grapple with the period following the Second World War, when full-fledged fluid modernity was introduced into the region, and how it unravelled. Pursuing very clear economic and political objectives, the United States sought to bolster an international governmental reason partly on the basis of a water apparatus.

2.1 Water and the colonisation of Palestine

During the first years of the British mandate over Palestine, a debate took place concerning the "Absorptive Capacity" of the land, meaning how many people it could carry. The question had implications for immigration and therefore became a crucial debate for the viability of the Zionist project. Using British assessments from the 1870s, Zionist leaders David Ben Gurion and Yitzhak Ben Zvi promoted their cause for massive Jewish immigration asserting that Palestine could easily support over 10 million people (Tal, 2017). From then on, plans and actions to provide sufficient land and water resources for an ever-increasing Jewish population were continuously made and remade.

Since the end of the 19th century, Zionist leaders had recognised that building a modern state with a developed economy in Palestine required privileged access to large volumes of water, not only land. In 1898, when Theodor Herzl asked the German Kaiser Wilhelm II to mediate with the Ottoman Sultan so that he would allow Jews to settle in Palestine, the European ruler noted that plenty of water would be needed for any massive immigration plan. Besides bolstering agricultural output, water resource development could also allow for hydropower generation to enable industrialisation (Shapland, 1997, 5–7; Dolatyar and Gray, 1999, 103–104). As for the British Crown, Lord Cromer convinced decision makers in London to reject early Zionist proposals, arguing that their schemes would require substantial water imports from the Nile

(Wolf, 1994, 10; Wolf, 1995, 16), affecting British interests in cotton-producing Egypt.

Between 1920 and 1923, Britain and France reached a compromise agreement through which the latter would get a League of Nations mandate to rule over Lebanon and Syria, and the former a parallel one to govern Palestine and Transjordan, following the general terms of war-time pacts. They also agreed to create a national Jewish home in Palestine, in line with another British commitment known as the Balfour Declaration.

In catering to this end, at the Versailles Peace Conference of 1919, water was taken into consideration in drawing the borders of Palestine. It would seem that during the earlier stages of the process, European powers had negotiated borders with little regard for water resources, but Zionists asked the British to take into account their interests vis-à-vis the fluid. They sought territory large enough to include not only biblical lands, but also strategic areas for military security and water resources for economic development (Wolf, 1994, 19–21; Wolf, 1995, 14). In its official statement to the Conference, the Zionist delegation campaigned to have sufficient land to the north to include the Litani River and Mount Hermon, to the south to cover the Negev desert and to the east of the Jordan River to encompass its eastern tributaries (see The Zionist Organization, 1919). See the location of these watercourses in Map 2.1.

However, it would have been impossible to accommodate these demands with the needs of the other key British allies with whom the Kingdom also had made territorial commitments, the French and the Hashemites. Hydro-strategic territories were distributed accordingly. To begin with, the Litani was to lie entirely within what was to become Lebanon. Most of Mount Hermon ended up in Syria and to an extent each of the three tributaries of the Upper Jordan would be in a different state—the Hasbani in Lebanon, the Dan in Palestine and the Banias in Syria. The rest of the Upper Jordan, most of the shore of Lake Tiberias and a small triangle of land between the lake, the lower Jordan and the Yarmuk River were within Palestine, as well as the West Bank of the Lower Jordan (Wolf, 1995, 26–28). The Hashemite Emirate of Transjordan was to lie east of the lower Jordan River, including its eastern tributaries and part of the southern bank of the Yarmuk River. Almost the entire northern part of the Yarmuk and all its tributaries were left within Syria.

Both the Zionist Organization and the Transjordanian government ordered several water resource development studies, carried out

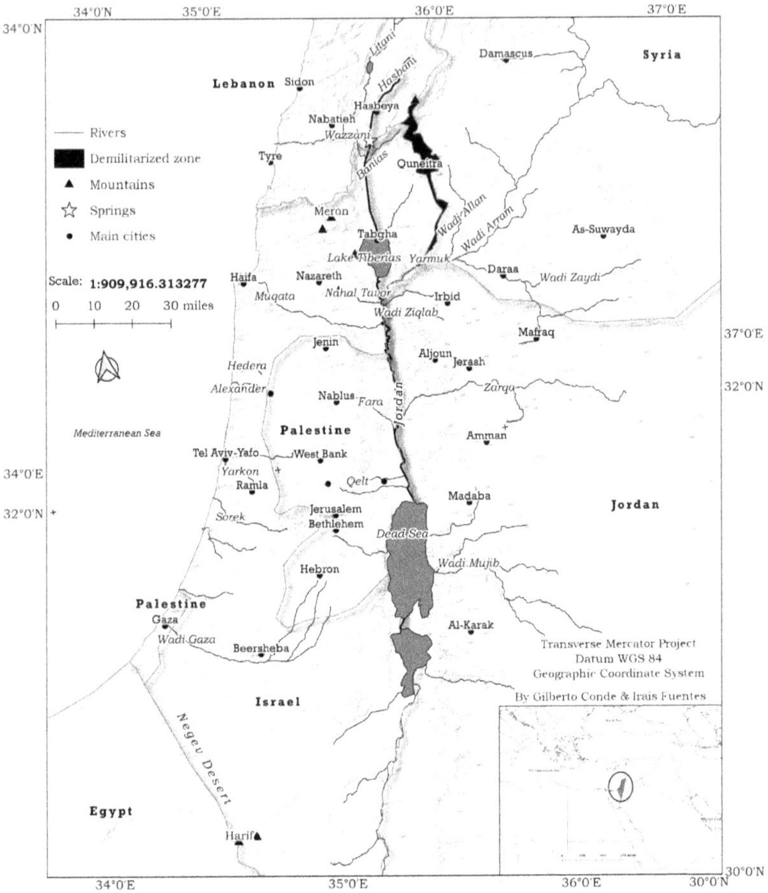

Map 2.1 The Jordan-Yarmuk River System. Map by the author and Iraís Fuentes.

between 1936 and 1948, aimed at guaranteeing economic development, which had to keep up with demographic projections. It will come as no surprise that these studies were mutually contradictory. The debate around the capacity of Palestine to admit massive immigration intensified anew in 1937. The growth of Jewish immigration into Palestine and its effects on the livelihoods of scores of Arab Palestinians had triggered a massive uprising the previous year that prompted Britain to establish a Royal Commission, headed by Lord Peel, to study ways of confronting the increasing instability. Its conclusions proposed the partition of Palestine into a Jewish and an Arab state. Discussions included proposals on borders and water resources to sustain a rapidly expanding population (Dodge and Tell, 1996, 171). Two years later, Michael Ionides, a British official working for the Transjordanian emirate, studied the possibility of developing the water resources of the region and concluded that they were too scant to sustain the Zionist plans (see, for example, Naff and Matson, 1984, 30–32; Lonergan and Brooks, 1994, 121–122). The proposals made by Ionides would serve as a basis for further Jordanian planning of water resources development on the Jordan and Yarmuk.

Meanwhile, according to Dodge and Tell (1996, 171), Zionists tended to exaggerate the potential for massive agricultural settlements based on Jordan River water resources by quoting unpublished studies and commanding new ones. Prompted by a group of Zionists, the US government commissioned Walter Clay Lowdermilk, from the Tennessee Valley Authority, to carry out a survey of the Jordan River Valley. In 1944, he concluded that 4 million Jews could be added to the local population on condition of developing both the Jordan and the Litani on a massive scale (Naff and Matson, 1984, 30–32; Wolf, 1995, 41–42; Lonergan, 2000, 123). In other words, Lowdermilk could only assert that water resources in Palestine were sufficient for the immigration schemes by including the water of a river located outside Palestine, the fully Lebanese Litani River.

This dry outlook worried Zionist leaders, who included water planning as a key element of their strategic thinking, although, needless to say, the liquid was never the sole element dear to them. Other criteria, such as land and economic and military concerns, were also essential. Aaron T. Wolf (1995, 43) has argued that water was not at all important in Israeli strategic planning in the war of 1948, when the state was proclaimed. He claims that military actions concentrated on securing the three areas allocated to the state of Israel by the UN General Assembly. A number of Israeli historians publishing since the 1980s and 1990s have shown, however, that official Israeli historiography is usually biased, and assertions such as these must be taken with caution.

Actually, the results of the 1948 war did have important implications from the water point of view, as well as the actions of Zionist armed organisations before and during the war. These organisations actively encouraged and promoted the exodus of terrorised Arabs from the lands in which they lived (see, *inter alia*, Pappé, 2006, 28).[1] They took the territory connecting the coastal regions to Jerusalem, as well as the Western parts of the city and as much extra-UN-allocated land as possible, biting into the drilling area of the western slope of the West

Bank Mountain Aquifer (see Map 3.1). Undoubtedly, several reasons contribute to explain why Zionists sought to achieve a large exodus of Arab Palestinians. Absorptive capacity, which was strongly related to water availability, must have been among them since one of their paramount aims was to bolster immigration. Creating the Palestinian refugee problem and conquering the territories in the drilling areas of the Mountain Aquifer would increase the water-related absorptive capacity to bring new immigrants into the land.

True, the achievements of the State of Israel in the war of 1948 implied only some gains in terms of water concerns. Many important hydro-strategic territories were left on the eastern side of the armistice Green Line. Moreover, the army of the recently created Syrian Republic managed to secure patches of land that had been part of mandatory Palestine, neighbouring what now had become the state of Israel, such as the hills overlooking the Banias Springs, a stretch of the Upper Jordan that includes the Hula Swamps, and a large part of the Yarmuk Triangle. While refusing to relinquish territory beyond the UN partition plan that they conquered through arms, Israeli leaders insisted on including in their state the lands that they had lost to the Syrians. When Syrian President Hosni al-Zaim made a generous, though domestically unpopular, peace offer to the Israelis in 1949, Israeli President Moshe Sharett rejected even meeting his Arab counterpart, arguing that he was not ready to accept losing the lands that his forces were unable to grab along the Jordan because the control over water was at stake (Sharett, quoted by Morris, 1990, 25–26). The areas under Syrian control but claimed by the Israelis were turned into demilitarised zones (DMZs). The parties had accepted that sovereignty over these territories would later be decided through a peace agreement (Neff, 1994, 26–40).

Undoubtedly, the main goal of Zionists in 1948 was to establish the state in as large an area as possible, which implied achieving a number of essential territorial goals. Nonetheless, the water-related absorptive capacity of what then became the State of Israel was expanded and later stretched even further through the development and control of most of the water resources in the area, including the Upper Jordan and the western drilling areas of the Mountain Aquifer in the West Bank, even though they lost some important areas from the hydro-strategic point of view. Since Israeli authorities decided that they would not allow the refugees to return to their homes, their exodus to neighbouring states shifted the pressure on resources, including, of course, water, from Israel to the West Bank and the neighbouring Arab states, some characterised by a scarcity of renewable water resources, especially Jordan.

Clearly, during the first half of the 20th century, water, as well as other resources in Palestine, had become a key subject of political modernity. Projects for large population transfers required large amounts of water as the fluid was necessary not only for direct consumption needs, but to make agricultural and even industrial jobs available for millions. The state of Israel and its precursors were thinking in what we can call biopolitical terms, seeking to ensure the availability of the resources that would guarantee the administration of life for their target population. These were the foundations of a nascent water apparatus that would help them guarantee a governmentality to woo Jewish populations from around the world into the state. The evolutions of the following years were to bolster fluid modernity even further.

2.2 The Tigris-Euphrates and European hegemony

After the First World War, Britain and France negotiated with Turkey, in the name of Syria and Iraq, several water arrangements concerning the Tigris and Euphrates water resources. Sub-regional politics were characterised by the military, economic and diplomatic superiority of the European powers, which implied that they had an important amount of leverage when dealing with Turkey. The mandatory powers signed or promoted several agreements among themselves or with Turkey committing the states under their control to a number of decisions that later, with independence, Syria and Iraq would reject as imposed on the back of their societies by colonialists. See the Tigris and Euphrates Rivers and their tributaries in Map 2.2.

The two European powers agreed that Syria would seek the agreement of Iraq before constructing any infrastructure that could significantly reduce the discharge of the Tigris and Euphrates. Since France and Britain had signed a water agreement with the Ottoman Empire in 1922, they had to get the Turkish Republic, once established, to ratify what had been negotiated with the Sublime Porte. France signed a Turkey-Syria good neighbourliness treaty in 1926 and another one in 1929. The final 1930 borders protocol between Turkey and France reiterates stipulations of previous accords whereby Turkey would let water flow through the Quwayq River to the Syrian city of Aleppo, and agree to supplement it with fluid from the Euphrates if necessary. In 1939, just as the Second World War was on the brink of breaking out, France surrendered the province of Alexandretta to Turkey. The two countries also agreed that Syria would share the Asi/Orontes waters with the now Turkish province. These agreements stopped being honoured in 1940, during the World War, and have been a source of mutual reproach

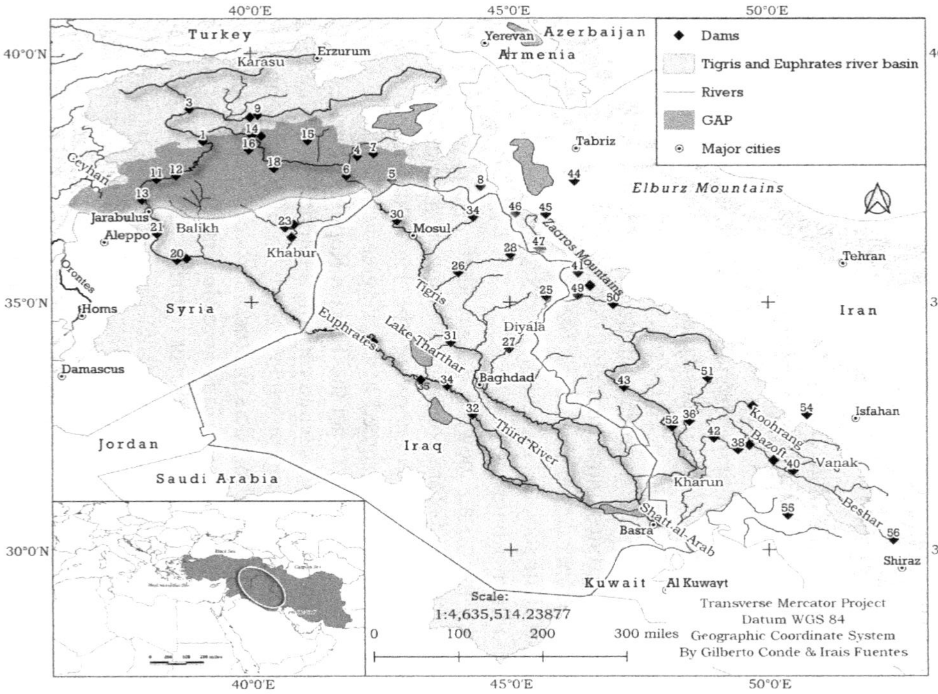

Turkey

No.	Dam name
1	Karakaya
2	Karkamis
3	Keban
4	Kiraziik
5	Sirnak
6	Ilisu
7	Cetin
8	Aslandag
9	Beyhan I
10	Beyhan II
11	Burç Bendi
12	Ataturk
13	Birecik
14	Kralkiza
15	Batman
16	Devegecidi
17	Dicle
18	Goksu

Iraq

No.	Dam name
29	Hamrin
30	Mosul
31	Samarra
32	Hindiya
33	Haditha
34	Fallujah
35	Ramadi-Habbaniyah

Iran

No.	Dam name
36	Dez
37	Abbaspouro
38	Masjed Soleyman
39	Karun 3
40	Karun 4
41	Garan
42	Gotvand
43	Seimare
44	Alavian
45	Mahabad
46	Silveh
47	Sardasht
48	Azad
49	Daryan
50	Gavshan
51	Eyvashan
52	Kakleh
53	Rudbar Lorestan
54	Zayanderud
55	Marun
56	Doroodzan

Syria

No.	Dam name
19	Baath
20	Tabaqa
21	Tishrine
22	Khabour
23	Hasake
24	Hasake Est

Iraq

No.	Dam name
25	Derbendikhan
26	Dibbis
27	Diyala
28	Dukan

Legend:
- ◆ Dams
- Tigris and Euphrates river basin
- Rivers
- GAP
- ⊙ Major cities

Transverse Mercator Project
Datum WGS 84
Geographic Coordinate System
By Gilberto Conde & Iraís Fuentes

Scale:
1:4,635,514.23877

0   100   200   300 miles

Map 2.2 The Tigris-Euphrates basin and dams. Map by the author and Iraís Fuentes.

between Turkey and Syria thereafter. While Turkish authors (such as Inan, 1994, 236) accuse the Syrian authorities of violating the 1939 compromise, the latter assert that France lacked the legitimacy to yield part of its territory to Turkey or any other country, not to mention that Turkey itself stopped abiding by the agreements.[2]

The Turkish Republic and the Kingdom of Iraq, formally independent since 1933, signed a neighbourly agreement in 1946 after the Second World War. The text included a protocol on the Tigris and Euphrates. Failure to implement it also has become a source of mutual recriminations between these two countries. The Turkish authorities were required to seek the consent of their Iraqi counterparts before undertaking infrastructure works on the rivers. The document also envisaged establishing observation posts and facilities in Turkey for flood control in Iraq, which the latter would pay. The fifth article stipulated that projects in the basin would be harmonised (Majzoub, 1994; Inan, 1994). Although the parties negotiated as independent states, which should oblige them to observe the provisions of the agreement, the document soon became a dead letter.

In short, during the mandate period, Turkey signed deals imposing obligations on itself to respect the water rights of the lower riparian countries. At the same time, it got significant concessions by playing on the European political chessboard, such as the annexation of the province of Alexandretta and gaining rights over the waters of the Orontes. Nonetheless, these negotiations also concealed a subordination of Ankara to the British and French mandates over Syria and Iraq, which were able to conduct asymmetrical negotiations over upstream riparian Turkey to obtain a guaranteed water flow.

At the time, the fluid modernity aspect of these agreements was more important for both France and Britain, as they needed at the same time to legitimise their rule over the territories they had under mandate and to be able to make them productive for the needs of their colonial economies. Even though the resources of these rivers would become important for Turkey in the later part of the century, during the first decades of the Republic, East and Southeast Anatolia were faraway regions not so crucial for economic development. In other words, they were busy developing the governmental reason and even fluid modernity in the West of the country. This, together with the fact that France and Britain were much stronger states, might have played a role in their accepting water agreements that could have been deemed favourable to their neighbours. Turkish leaders usually showed a different negotiating attitude when territory was at stake, a core part of their nationalist perspective.

2.3 Cold War, the Nile and the Jordan River

As the Cold War was starting to develop in the late 1940s and early 1950s, US officials sought to establish a governmental reason in the oil-rich Middle East. This meant securing the integration of the region in the Western Bloc, which meant keeping it at distance from the Eastern Bloc. The overall circumstances, however, were complex, as the social environment was extremely agitated. Some of the countries had just achieved independence in a rather hectic way. The State of Israel, replacing the British mandate over Palestine, was established in 1948 over an extension of land that greatly exceeded what the United Nations had provided in its Resolution 181 of 29 November 1947. These events translated into widespread suspicion in the Arab street of what the postcolonial order would bring. The entire region was awash with nationalism. The US State Department sought to offer an alternative to the colonial past but had to juggle many simultaneous concerns, which included a normalisation of Arab-Israeli relations. Interestingly, the strategy put forth by US President Dwight D. Eisenhower and Secretary of State John Foster Dulles to achieve US objectives centred on fluid modernity. It seemed as if they wanted to establish an international governmental reason based to a large extent on a water apparatus.

The Eisenhower Administration made efforts to woo Egypt to its policy through funding for hydraulic projects. In 1952, a republican revolution ended the Egyptian Monarchy as well as a previously more or less unquestioned subjection to Britain. Gamal Abdel Nasser, leader of the recently established Republic, longed to develop a modern, successful and independent state but was conscious of the limitations imposed by the geopolitical context of his time. When the State Department and the IBRD approached him with a multi-million-dollar loan proposal to build a High Dam at Aswan to replace the one built by the British at the turn of the century, transforming it into the centrepiece of Egyptian economic development (Waterbury, 1979, 102–103), Nasser was understandably interested. Hydropower and the ability to reclaim more land for agriculture through irrigation promised to boost his development plans, his biopolitics over a rapidly growing population and, therefore, his governmentality. However, there was a catch. Explicitly or not, the condition was to take a leading role in incorporating other Arab countries into the Cold War military mechanism that the Western Bloc wanted to establish in the Middle East as well as leading Lebanon, Syria and Jordan in negotiating and signing a water deal with Israel.

The years after the war had witnessed a sharp increase in water consumption both in Israel and Transjordan, not to mention the demographic projections estimated by the experts who had drafted revised plans. Now that the British had left along with their restrictions, Israel actively encouraged Jewish immigration. Irrigated agriculture was a relatively easy way to make jobs available for the newcomers (Naff and Matson, 1984, 30–32) as compared with the investments required to make enough industrial jobs available to keep up with demographic growth. Shortly after the 1948 war, Israeli leaders came to the conclusion that the main limitation to agricultural development was water rather than land (Kally, 1993, 21). The Zionist Organisation hired Walter C. Lowdermilk, a US expert, to work out the engineering details of a plan that eventually bore his name. All water resources in Israel were to be connected into a single three-meter-diameter National Water Carrier that would provide the fluid to all the cities and allow for the development of irrigation all the way to the Negev desert.

Simultaneously, water demand in Jordan rose abruptly in response to the arrival of hundreds of thousands of Palestinian refugees. The US and British administrations prompted Jordan, as well as Syria, Lebanon and Egypt, to settle the refugees in their countries for good (Dodge and Tell, 1996, 175–176), thereby yielding to the Israeli refusal to allow the Palestinians to return to their homes and lands. This meant that refugees needed not only aid for everyday needs, but also permanent jobs and housing. Proposals were made for the UN Relief and Works Agency for Palestine Refugees in the Near East (UNRWA) to conceive and build water infrastructure so as to develop large agricultural projects to employ the refugees. M. E. Bunger, a US engineer working with the Technical Cooperation Agency, was sent to conceive a development plan for the entire basin. The UNRWA approved it in 1953 and committed 20% of its budget to the scheme.

After reaching an agreement, Jordan and Syria began building a reservoir at Maqarin to tackle their power and water needs (Shapland, 1997, 14–15), but diplomacy blocked their progress. Representatives of Israel campaigned against the project in Washington and managed to block the funding (Dodge and Tell, 1996, 177–178). The Eisenhower Administration, however, had something else in mind for water in the region, which might have played a role in making the decision.

Soon after the 1948 war, Israeli authorities implemented actions to control water and capture more territory. First, they sought to control some of the sources of Jordan River waters that lay in the DMZs, the disputed lands with Syria, which technically were within the boundaries of the latter. The Israelis initiated a number of projects in the DMZs in order to gradually claim the territories as theirs and eventually conquer them back from Syria. Most notoriously, they proceeded to draining the

Hula Swamps and later building an intake to withdraw Upper Jordan waters for the National Water Carrier at Banat Ya'qub Bridge, just south of the Swamps. By then, they were proceeding with the construction of the Carrier with US funding. It was a challenge to the Syrians, since both the Swamps and the bridge were inside lands conquered by its army during the war. Developing infrastructure there equated to claiming ownership of the area. Armed Israeli farmers were also sent to settle in and till the lands. All this triggered several skirmishes between Israeli and Syrian forces. Although the UN Security Council turned down a Syrian objection to the Israeli drying of the Swamps in 1951, a Soviet veto later turned down a pro-Israeli proposal to allow making the intake for the Water Carrier at the bridge area.

Perhaps with several simultaneous aims, the US State Department decided to intervene with a certain neutrality to oppose the independent fluid modernity initiatives underway and promote a proposal of its own for the entire area. The idea had been simmering in the State Department for a few years, as is clearly shown in declassified documents that explicitly asserted that water was capable of luring the Arabs into recognising Israel and bowing to US leadership (Horner, 1948, 898–901). In an already heated Cold War context, the US administration understood that a total bias in favour of Israel would certainly throw the Arabs into Soviet arms.

The Administration promoted a process of intense though indirect negotiations for the distribution of water among the states of the Jordan River Basin. For Arab-Israeli water negotiations to begin, the White House needed to force the Israeli government to participate. As of November 1953, the Israelis were still refusing to abide by the Security Council resolution that required them to remove the water intake from the DMZ. The US government threatened to suspend funding for the Carrier if Israel failed to immediately comply (Naff and Matson, 1984, 35–39). Only then was the intake moved 13 km south to the shores of Lake Tiberias. Authors such as Wolf (1995, 45) argue that the Israelis paid a high cost for this, as water is more saline in Lake Tiberias, and the topography requires a high energy input to pump the water up into the Water Carrier. The move, nonetheless, also had advantages. Allowing Upper Jordan water into Tiberias has saved the Lake from increased salinity by turning it into the main surface-water reservoir of Israel.

In October 1953, Eisenhower appointed Eric Johnston Special Ambassador to negotiate an Arab-Israeli water agreement. Dulles, in his report to the President after a visit to the area in June, had stressed not only the importance of the region for its oil resources but also the dire need for developing water resources. He concluded, in line with the 1948 document cited before, that it was possible to use this issue to seduce Arabs and Israelis into establishing cooperative relations (Hillel, 1994, 159–161). Johnston managed to get the parties to accept a water-sharing scheme and clearly defined terms for water resource development but abandoned his mediating role before getting the agreement ratified. By July 1955, after two years of shuttle diplomacy, coming and going with proposals and counter proposals, the Special Ambassador had produced a Unified Plan, better known as the Johnston Plan, which attended to the concerns of the co-riparian countries. The plan gave the Hashemite Kingdom of Jordan 720 hm³/y, 100 of which were to come from the Upper Jordan, Syria 132 of which 42 came from the Jordan, and Lebanon 35. Israel would take the remainder—estimated variously at 400–450 hm³/y—of which, 25 came from the Yarmuk.

The context surrounding these negotiations is crucial to understand why so much progress was made, why the parties refused to sign the resulting document and why the US administration stopped pressing for its adoption after having invested so much in promoting it. Through the Arab League, President Nasser had been encouraging Arab leaders in the watershed to participate in the talks, hoping to convince Eisenhower that he was a valuable partner, while expecting funding for the development projects in his country. Nasser understood it was impossible to obtain an IBRD loan without US approval. Indeed, the Bank administration had been temporising the approval seeking to obtain an even clearer Egyptian engagement with the Western alliance and US leadership.

Paradoxically, it was precisely Western pressures that led Nasser to move away. Nonetheless, his distancing from Washington might have further enhanced Nasser's rising position as leader of the Arab street, which was experiencing, as mentioned before, growing nationalist and anti-imperialist feelings. A radical shift took place in the mind of Nasser and other Arab leaders over the course of 1955. Britain—which had ruled most of the region through different mechanisms, including pacts that guaranteed its continued military presence—Turkey, the only NATO member in the Middle East, and then Western-aligned Iraq signed a military alliance, the Baghdad Pact, on 24 February. The Arab public and several states saw the Pact as an instrument for imperialist control of the entire region. Four days later, Israeli forces crossed the armistice lines to raid an Egyptian military camp in the Gaza Strip, killing dozens of Egyptian soldiers. In spite of international condemnation of the raid, the United States refused to sell weapons to Egypt, and Nasser threatened to buy them from the Soviet Bloc. Dulles replied that, given the importance of Middle Eastern oil, a move of the sort would be unacceptable (Gerges, 1994, 34). These developments pushed Egyptian and Syrian leaders in an increasingly nationalist direction. In April, Indonesian President Sukarno hosted the Egyptian and Syrian presidents together with Jawaharlal Nehru from India, Zhou Enlai from China and leaders of two dozen other mainly Asian and African countries in the Bandung Conference, giving birth to "neutralism", what eventually would become the Non-Aligned Movement. This same month, the IBRD Technical Committee decided that Egypt had to adopt a strict fiscal policy to get the High Dam loan (Waterbury, 1979, 102–103), which was bound to remind any Egyptian of the British fiscal (and of course military) intervention of 1881.

The Johnston negotiation process continued through the summer, but ultimately collapsed. In July 1955, while seriously considering a Soviet military aid treaty, Nasser continued canvassing the Arab League on behalf of the Johnston scheme, perhaps still hoping for a breakthrough with the United States, as he knew that a weapons deal with the Eastern Bloc would break the relationship with Washington. It took a few months for Nasser and recently elected Syrian President Shukri al-Quwatli, who was also refused US military aid, to part ways with the Western Bloc. Israelis balked at having international supervision over the agreement, and the cabinet failed to ratify it. In October, instead of sanctioning the Plan, the Arab League opted to postpone a decision and sent it back to the Technical Committee for further study (Naff and Matson, 1984, 39–42). Nasser and al-Quwatli knew that ratifying the Unified Plan meant recognising the State of Israel without having negotiated fixed borders nor the fate of Palestinian refugees, among other important issues. That same month the Egyptian government reached a Soviet arms deal through Czechoslovakia to improve its defence capabilities.

For the US Administration, this response negated a key part of the governmental reason purpose of the Johnston mission, namely to attach Arab states to the Western Bloc and keep the Soviet Union at bay. Rather than softening its position, the State Department hardened it. The Special Envoy cancelled his mission and the parties never ratified the water plan. Nevertheless, the Unified Plan has since been greeted as a non-official accord, given that all the parties expressed their "technical" agreement with its provisions. Every now and then, the leaders of the co-riparian countries explicitly or implicitly refer to it when discussing Jordan-Yarmuk waters. Moreover, often the parties boast respecting its stipulations or accuse another of breaching them. While authors such as Hillel (1994, 161) and Wolf (1995, 23) have asserted that Israel has complied with the agreement,[3] Lonergan and Brooks (1994,

123) observe that this was only the case until 1967. It also has been employed by international organisations to make other plans, such as the Chase T. Main UNRWA proposal, which seeks to take into consideration both Arab and Israeli concerns (Naff and Matson, 1984, 39–42).

During its first years, the Eisenhower Administration introduced full-fledged fluid modernity in the Middle East with the hope of establishing an international governmental reason that securely incorporated in the Western Bloc the Arab states that had recently attained independence. Although full-fledged fluid modernity got firmly established in the region, the US governmental reason scheme failed, and it did so essentially because the colonialist mindset was still too deeply rooted among the leaders of core capitalist countries. Eisenhower, Dulles, British Prime Minister Winston Churchill and Foreign Secretary Anthony Eden dealt with Arab leaders Nasser and al-Quwatli as if they could use the mirage of water diplomacy and money for dams and other infrastructure to force the Arab leaders into accepting virtually any role chosen for them. It was impossible that this could work. It went against the spirit of the times. For the water apparatus to be effective, it would also have had to include giving at least a resemblance of pride for the Arab countries so that they too could have strengthened their domestic governmental reason. US diplomacy was conducted on the basis of a culture of imperial arrogance at a time when decolonisation was taking place and virtually everyone in most Arab countries had personally endured the grievances of colonialism just a few years before.

2.4 Cold War, the Asi and the Euphrates

US and World Bank efforts to introduce full-fledged fluid modernity were aimed at the entire Arab Middle East. They started making a proposal to Syria, later extended it to Egypt and the other riparian countries of the Jordan-Yarmuk and soon reached out to Turkey and Iraq as well. In 1950, Syria was offered an IBRD loan for the development of the Ghab Swamps on the basin of the Asi/Orontes River. This watercourse rises in the Beqaa Valley within Lebanese territory, flows along a south-north trajectory, passing through the Syrian cities of Homs and Hama, bathing the Ghab valley before crossing westward into Alexandretta, or Hatay, which, readers will remember, France yielded to Turkish sovereignty in 1939. Agriculture has been extremely important along the banks of the Asi and the Ghab Valley in particular, becoming the breadbasket of Syria. While Eric Johnston was trying to strike a water deal among Jordan-Yarmuk riparian states, and Western countries were still considering whether to issue Egypt a loan to build the Aswan High Dam, Western creditors gave a nod to the Ghab project in spite of Turkish complaints (IBRD, 1955, 45–46).

In 1955, while this loan was being discussed and the Johnston mission was still underway, the Syrian government applied with the Bank to finance the Youssef Pasha Project on the Euphrates River to harness its waters for agricultural development. With the political climate as it was, the IBRD decided that the Youssef Pasha plan should wait until after the Ghab Marshes Project had been concluded, well into the 1960s. The bank argued that the reason for the decision was to avoid burdening the Syrian government with an excessive debt (IBRD, 1955). In an apparent turnabout, the following year, the Bank proposed a tripartite Turkish-Syrian-Iraqi Water Council to promote the joint utilisation of the river (see account by IBRD official Raj Krishna, 1995, 32). Although leaders of the three countries concurred that this was a logical aim, it failed to materialise. In order to participate in the tripartite council, Ankara demanded that all water matters in its relations with Syria be included, meaning the Asi River. If the Syrian authorities had agreed, they tacitly would have recognised Turkish sovereignty over Alexandretta, which Damascus refused to accept (Majzoub, 1994, 207). It seems quite obvious that the goal of the Turkish Adnan Menderes Administration was to obtain indirect Syrian recognition of Turkish sovereignty over Hatay/Alexandretta with the signature of a water agreement on the Asi, following a logic similar to what Johnston was trying to apply through Jordan-Yarmuk negotiations, to get Arab countries to recognise Israel tacitly.

Just like with Egypt, as discussed in the following section, the IBRD took the loan proposals off the table. For the US State Department and the Turkish Ministry of Foreign Affairs, the Damascus and Cairo purchase of Eastern Bloc weapons excluded them from participating in the Baghdad Pact or any other Cold War military mechanism led by the West. Syria had put itself on the opposite side of the icy trenches of geopolitics. The United States vetoed giving development support to Syria as well, which nonetheless pursued its projects, albeit with domestic resources and Soviet loans (Naff and Matson, 1984, 118–121). Thereafter, relations further deteriorated with the Turkish threat to invade Syria in 1957 and Iraq in 1958.

2.5 Aswan and the war of 1956

The War of Suez constituted the closing chapter in the introduction of full-fledged fluid modernity into the Middle East. Although triggered by the Egyptian nationalisation of the Suez Canal, the 1956 British, French and Israeli war on Egypt was a late colonial war. Its inception, however, was related to the failure of the United States to establish a governmental reason on the basis of its fluid-modernity plans. The State Department had hoped to make the Arab leaders discipline themselves and accept the postcolonial order that the Western Bloc was preparing for them. The plan, as we have seen, was at least partly based on establishing an enticing water apparatus lubricated with millions of dollars for hydro-infrastructural investments in the spirit of the TVA. After its collapse, Nasser sought alternative ways of continuing with the bolstering of the water apparatus for the sake of domestic biopolitics, of administering life in Egypt, by developing hydropower and water resources from the Nile.

The US government decided to block the IBRD funding for the Aswan High Dam as Egypt was following its own script. Once Nasser reached the conclusion late in 1955 that Egypt had no option but to buy weapons from the Eastern Bloc and acted accordingly, in March of the following year, the US State Department produced and the President approved a top secret Memorandum, code named "Omega", which aimed at marginalising Nasser, apparently hoping to push him back into compliance. The first two policy recommendations directly regarding Egypt read, "1. Export licences covering arms shipments to Egypt, whether from Governmental or private sources, *will continue to be denied.* 2. The US and the UK *will continue to delay* the conclusion of current negotiations on the High Aswan Dam" (emphasis added).[4] Although these two lines offer enough material to teach an entire class on Cold War politics, the goal here is to draw attention to their fluid modernity aspect. The State Department was still hoping to use water and water-related investments as an instrument of politics to try to force the Egyptian leadership into its governmental reason project in the region.

The second page of the memorandum, however, brings forth an aspect of power at odds with biopower in the development of the international governmental reason, inclined to repression. The first policy recommendation towards "other countries" reads,

1. The US and the UK will commence negotiations with the Sudan with a view to developing a situation of influence in that country which would minimize Egyptian influence and its control of the head waters of the Nile.

Although uncertain, other points in the memorandum, particularly number 5, regarding Ethiopia, could have been drafted with similar fluid modernity ideas in mind. While biopower commonly refers to the management of life, in a state of emergency it shifts to the administration of death, as an extreme means of discipline and control. It occurred to US leaders that, as engineer Jeff Thompson fancied (see epigraph to Chapter 1), they could intervene in the Nile, not to make the river finer or less so, but to discipline Egypt.

With nationalism still on the rise, the Arab street demanded Nasser reject the imposition of conditions from Washington and London. When the IBRD refused to grant the loan to build the High Dam, the Nasser Administration, by then fully immersed in fluid modernity, nationalised the Suez Canal to gather the necessary funds to pay for the development plans that Egypt was contemplating. Britain and France, owners of the Canal, together with Israel, attacked Egypt but failed to discuss their concerted plans with Washington. In agreement with the Soviet Union, the United States stepped in to stop the offensive and contain the damage that the attack wrought upon the Western Bloc in the Arab Middle East. It was then, according to Kolko (2006), that the White House decided to finish the process of replacing Britain as the power in charge of coordinating and conducting Western interests in the region.

In January 1957, Eisenhower made public his own doctrine for the Middle East, seeking to limit Soviet access and undermine the support that nationalist governments were receiving from the Soviet Union, both through military and development aid, exactly what the US government had denied Nasser just a few months before. With US approval, Israel chose to cultivate relations with what it called the "periphery" of Arab countries, which meant boosting relations with Turkey, Iran and Ethiopia, as well as with minorities within the Arab world (Alpher, 2015).

2.6 Conclusions

In the Middle East, as in the rest of the world, fluid modernity arrived to stay. Already in the 19th century and early 20th century, the Ottoman Empire began building and restoring water infrastructure in some of its territories according to its rationale. The European powers that ruled many of these territories with a colonial logic after the First World War furthered the fluid modernity logic and strove to guarantee the flow of water with biopolitics and capitalist objectives. This also happened with the Zionist colonisers of Palestine, although with a twist. They were building a permanent settler colonial project that required—or at least they believed it demanded—the administration of life and water in priority for those for whom they were building the state, whether already living in the territory or being expected to arrive later. This meant restricting native Palestinians' access to the fluid.

Full-fledged fluid modernity was introduced in the early 1950s by a conscious act of US administrations, which actively sought to develop an international mechanism capable of strengthening a US-led governmental reason. In it, leaders of the countries that recently had achieved independence, led by Egypt, could find sufficient material incentives to discipline themselves, finding their place in the Western Bloc, which implied keeping the Soviet Union at bay and coming to terms with the state of Israel. The scheme was clumsily put into action and finally failed between 1955 and 1956, when Nasser and other nationalist leaders realised that the role that they were being assigned in the fledgling governmentality was one of neocolonials that had to accept humiliation and foreign ascendancy over their development plans. As will be seen in the following chapter, the complimentary side of biopolitics, that of repression, reserved for situations of emergency, was then considered for the water apparatus, by continuing to deny loans for dams, cancelling water agreements and seeking to control the headwaters of rivers.

Notes

1 Even the most pro-Israel of the New Israeli Historians have agreed on this account of the facts.
2 With Turkish irrigation programs, the Quwayq dried out in the 1960s. In the 2000s, however, its sources were supplemented with transfers from the Euphrates.
3 Haddadin (1996), a Jordanian scholar, ambiguously asserts that Israel and Jordan have complied "to a certain extent".
4 US Department of State / Foreign relations of the United States (FRUS), 1955–1957. Arab-Israeli dispute, 1 January–26 July 1956 (1955–1957), p. 419 and ff. https://digital.library.wisc.edu/1711.dl/S3RKQGHILZFYM8T.

3 Fluid modernity in coercive mode

The Suez War of 1956 was a turning point and, in many ways, represented a defeat of Imperialism. The leaders of the Western Bloc were forced to rethink the method of unilaterally imposing the terms of the postcolonial order. During the following years, the contest over the boundaries of state sovereignty persisted. Domestic and international water apparatuses continued to be established, although often differing from those originally hoped for by their initial enthusiastic promoters, i.e., the White House, the World Bank and large US construction corporations. Within states, the water apparatus, centred around water administration, also served as a mechanism of consensus, at least for the section of the population of each state considered to be fully part of the nation. However, in the international, among-states arena, the stronger ones had a rougher time, at least temporarily, in establishing regional, basin-wide water apparatuses as means to obtain flexible terms of sovereignty from the weaker countries.

From the 1960s through the 1980s, each state in the Middle East built its own water infrastructure and water ideology with the aid of a different set of world powers, either from the Western Bloc or the Eastern Bloc. Usually, they paid little attention to the effects that their damming activity had on co-riparian countries. In the Tigris and Euphrates basin, some did propose, in several instances, integrated basin-wide management schemes. On occasion, they even seem to have meant it. In others, it was merely token negotiation proposals.

The countries capable of commanding more resources used them in different ways. When possible, they exploited their ability to retain water in reservoirs to discipline neighbouring countries or employed their military and diplomatic might to get more of the fluid from a shared watercourse. This coercive course of action was often complemented with negotiations and sometimes with agreements. When the accent was put on bare power relations, this could simply be understood as a shift

DOI: 10.4324/9781003356905-4

in biopolitics from the administration of life to that of death to compel co-riparian states into compliance on water or non-water related issues. Individuals may agree to self-impose discipline and accept hierarchical power, especially in arrangements which they feel as part of biopolitics. States, however, even weak ones, may more easily opt to resist. Some sub-altern social groups, especially those openly excluded from biopolitics and the governmental reason, such as oppressed nationalities, have also shown an ability to resist.

The terms of the international governmental reason that US administrations proposed for the Middle East and other places were more openly stated after the Suez crisis. As discussed in Chapter 2, during the inaugural period of full-fledged fluid modernity, the distribution of water-apparatus benefits was one of the foremost mechanisms, together with other infrastructure-related programmes, promoted by the United States and its allies to achieve a pliant postcolonial order in the Middle East (and in the rest of the postcolonial world). The 1957 Eisenhower doctrine made explicit that development aid would be distributed mostly to countries that aligned with US policies. As will be remembered from the end of Chapter 2, some Middle East allies of the United States that already wielded tremendous power with huge US military aid, Israel, Turkey and Iran, had come together in an "alliance of the periphery". These countries often took a hostile stance towards neutralist states in the region, Egypt and Syria, as well as Iraq after its 1958 republican revolution.

This chapter explores the evolutions of water politics in the Jordan River and Mountain Aquifer basins and in the Tigris and Euphrates basin in terms of fluid modernity and the governmental reason in the period spanning from 1956 to 1990. During this period, interstate tensions were commonly high in the region. Therefore, hydropolitics took place in an often-aggressive environment, in which the Soviet Union tried to moderate the frictions among its allies, and the United States sought to weaken the secularist nationalist Arab states. The chapter first summarises the complex political situation in the region, and then deals with the Arab-Israeli water conflict before moving to the one involving Turkey, Syria and Iraq, and the Kurds.

3.1 The Middle East political context

The workings of the water apparatus on the international scale have been contingent upon the ups and downs of international politics and economics. Although it would be difficult to summarise the context in which it operated in a few paragraphs, readers should keep in mind some of its general features. The 1960s in the Middle East were years of nationalism and radicalisation. Arab nationalists were inclined to socialism, as radical change seemed a requisite to achieve thorough emancipation from open or disguised colonialism. The Palestine Liberation Organisation (PLO) was founded in 1964 by the Arab League. Young Palestinians were taking up arms to become Fedayeen and frequently raided the territories of Palestine-turned Israel. A period of inter-Arab Cold War ensued (Kerr, 1967), in which Western-allied conservative, mostly monarchical and often Islamist, regimes, such as Saudi Arabia, Kuwait and Jordan, competed with neutralist nationalist, mostly secularist, progressive republics, Egypt, Syria and Iraq.

Everything seemed possible to the nationalists, as they enjoyed the favour of the streets even in rival states. Perhaps in some way this optimism led Arab nationalist currents to oppose each other. After a short-lived experience of Arab unity with the unification of Egypt and Syria into the United Arab Republic (UAR), some of the more successful nationalists entrenched themselves in their own states, at the apparent cost of postponing the ideal to unify the Arab nation in a single political entity. Nasser came to abominate the Syrians; the Baath fractured into a left and right wing, and Egypt was bogged down in war-ravaged Yemen in a confrontation with Western-backed Saudi Arabia.

Turkey took a slight distance from the Western alliance, although far from foregoing its allegiance to it. After nationalist and secularist military officers staged a military coup in 1960, they were made to feel important when Washington stationed nuclear-warhead-loaded Jupiter missiles in their territory. But they felt utterly dispensable when in 1962 the White House and the Kremlin negotiated to withdraw their missiles from Turkey and Cuba, respectively, without consulting with their local allies. When Turkish confidence in the Western alliance suffered again two years later in relation to the Cyprus crisis, Ankara opted to improve its diplomatic interactions with the Soviet Union and with Arab countries, although taking care not to threaten its connections with Washington and Tel Aviv.

The context started to change rapidly after 1967. Israel, allied with the United States and the West, strove to vanquish Arab nationalism. Its efforts culminated in the June 1967 war, when, with the aid of US intelligence, it defeated several Arab armies in a very short period of time. It occupied the West Bank and Gaza, the territories of Palestine that had remained Arab after 1948, as well as the Egyptian Sinai and the Syrian Golan heights. In its state form, Arab nationalism took a severe blow with the 1967 defeat. Nonetheless, the Hashemite Monarchy of Jordan, tightly associated with the Western powers, had to move diligently, as a large part of its population was Palestinian and Arab nationalist. Conservative monarchies reconciled with the radical republics, but by the turn of the decade, more conservative figures took the reins of power in each of Egypt, Syria and Iraq.

In 1973, Cairo and Damascus achieved a relative victory as they coordinated an offensive against Israel to recover their lost territories. The Israeli state deployed enormous efforts to neutralise the Palestine Liberation Organization, which was established in several Arab countries, particularly in Jordan, from where guerrillas entered to fight what they still saw as an illegitimate occupation. Israel put military pressure on Jordan to placate the Palestinians, who were massacred in what has come to be known as Black September, 1970. The PLO then moved its offices to Lebanon. Israel made several interventions in Lebanon until it invaded the country in 1982, forcing the Organisation to move its headquarters to distant Tunisia. The Israeli forces remained in South Lebanon until 2000.

The occupation of the West Bank and Gaza meant that Israel came to govern a sizeable Palestinian population, which increasingly resisted the military occupation rule. In 1987, the Palestinians in the West Bank and Gaza started an unarmed uprising that has come down in history as the First Intifada.

The Turkish military staged a second coup in 1971 and a third one in 1980, as ultra-nationalist and Islamic fundamentalist militants clashed with leftist students and unionists in the streets. Kurdish organisations were becoming increasingly active, denouncing the discrimination against Kurds. They aspired to establish their own state as the only way out of oppression. In 1978, a small group of Socialist students founded the Kurdistan Workers' Party (PKK), the leaders of which managed to avoid arrest during the 1980 coup and fled to Syria, where they received political asylum. After establishing training camps in Lebanon, they began an armed uprising against the Turkish state in 1984. In the 1960s and the 1970s, Kurds in Iraq had also been fighting for autonomy and even for an independent state through the Kurdistan Democratic Party (KDP) and the splinter Patriotic Union of Kurdistan (PUK).

At the time, different states gave support to diverse armed groups. The United States, Israel and Iran, still under Mohammed Reza Pahlevi Shah, gave support to the Kurds in Iraq. Egypt and Iraq supported the PLO, while Syria, by then governed by Hafiz al-Asad, aided some of its member organisations, as well as the PKK. Iraq, where Saddam Hussein was calling the shots, and Jordan supported armed Islamic fundamentalist groups operating inside Syria. Turkey was a key US ally in the region, holding strategic military connections with Israel and Iran.

In 1979, a new regional geopolitical earthquake occurred when the Pahlavi dynasty was overthrown by a people's uprising and Shi'i clerics took the reigns of political power by establishing the Islamic Republic of Iran. Seeking to become the leader of the Arab world, Saddam Hussein got Iraq involved in a war with Iran, defending his own interests and those of the oil-rich Sunni monarchs of the Gulf, as well as the West.

3.2 Flexing the muscle over the Jordan River

In the years between the wars of 1956 and 1967, Israel and the Arab states worked hard on water-related initiatives to impose a reality of water sharing quotas on the ground in the Jordan River and Mountain Aquifer basins (see Map 3.1), either defending or revising the near agreements approved by the technical committees of the parties under the Johnston negotiations. Clashes and fighting did take place during this period with important effects for the distribution of water. Although water was perhaps not the foremost issue at stake, the fluid was certainly at the core of discourses and actions. In any case, an entirely modified water apparatus resulted, in which Israel got the lion's share.

Once the Johnston mission was aborted, Israel resumed, with US funding, building its Water Carrier to divert Upper Jordan waters to its entire territory, threatening to abstract more than the allocation agreed to by the Technical Committees during the negotiations. Arab states had to respond. In 1959, the Arab League started discussing how to tackle the challenge. While one side proposed the use of military force to prevent the completion of the Carrier, Nasser and the Jordanian monarchy opposed this idea, arguing that it would throw world opinion against them, and Israeli leaders could stage an attack while claiming to be reacting in self-defence (Mohammad Hasanein Heikal, *Sanawāt al-Ghalyān*, cited by Mukhayam and Hijazi, 1996, 131–132).[1] Instead, the 1964 Arab summit decided to act defensively and divert the Johnston-defined Arab share of the headwaters of the Banias and Hasbani. The plan was to carve up a canal through the Golan Heights to carry the liquid to the Yarmuk, to be stored behind a dam at Maqarin and from there give Jordan its share.

Although scholars have debated whether the Arab Diversion Plan would have abstracted more than the Arab share, some pro-Western and even pro-Israeli sources agree that it sought to divert only the Johnston negotiated Arab allocation. A 1962 US Central Intelligence Agency (CIA) study concluded that the Arab scheme would have withdrawn 125 hm³/y of water, less than the total Arab allocation (cited by Wolf, 1994, 24–26; Wolf, 1995, 49–51), which coincides with the 35%

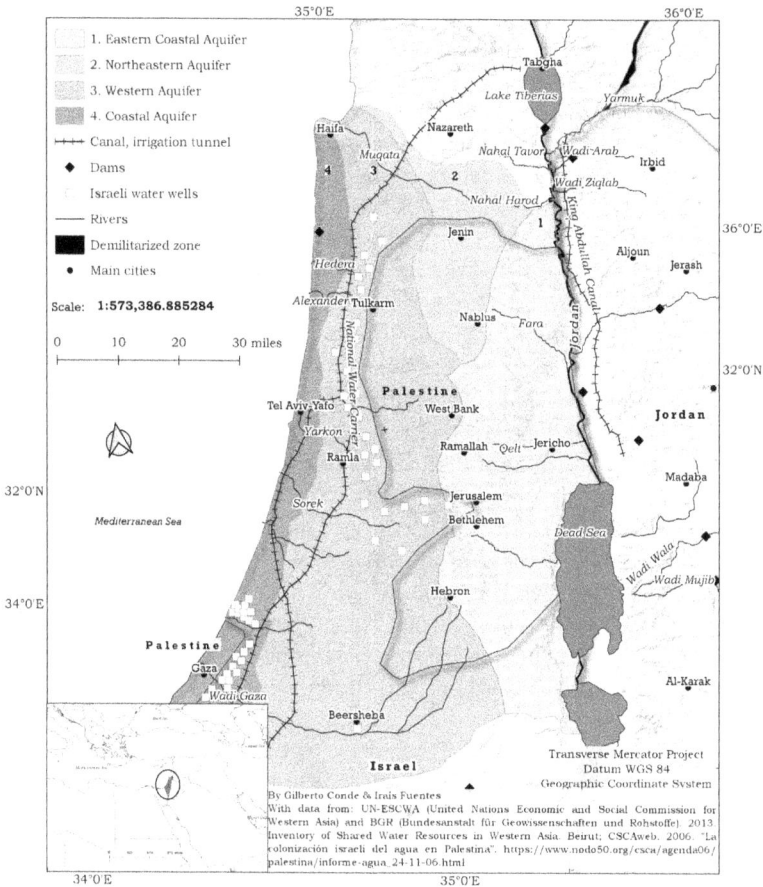

Map 3.1 Near East aquifers and water infrastructure. Map by the author and Iraís Fuentes.

of the total mentioned by Naff and Matson (1984, 43–44). Hof (2000, 150–167) and Soffer (1999, 167), however, claim that the Arab diversion project would have reduced the flow into the Carrier by 50 to 70%. This, it should be said, does not necessarily mean that the Arabs would have infringed their agreed quota. Conversely, failure to build the Arab Canal meant depriving Jordan of 100 hm^3 of Upper Jordan water per year from its Unified-Plan allocation. Financial problems notwithstanding, the works for the Arab Canal began in 1965.

The Israeli leadership decided to thwart the plan and threatened the Arab countries with war if they went on. US President Lyndon Johnson backed Israel and had his Cairo Ambassador deliver a letter to President Nasser stating that the Arab Canal constituted a grave threat to peace (Heikal, *Al-Infijār 1967*, cited by Mukhayam and Hijazi, 1996, 131–132). From March through August 1965, Israeli forces shelled the Arab works, and Lebanon stopped digging in July (Wolf, 1994, 24–26). Israeli hostility continued until April 1967, when construction sites well inside Syria were targeted (Naff and Matson, 1984, 43–44). The Arab League stopped working on the project, never to pick it up again.

Can it be said, given that Israeli forces shelled the Arab Canal in April 1967, that water was among the main goals of the Israeli offensive two months later, in the June war? While authors such as Bulloch and Darwish (1993, 34) and Klare (2001, 165 and ff.) support this thesis, others, including Wolf (1995, 72–75); Wolf (2000, 85–90); and Soffer (1999, 170), contend that the water ingredient had no role in the planning of the offensive and that its role was only indirect. To substantiate their claim, these authors argue that the strategy followed by the Israeli military command indicates that water was not a key concern. They first invaded the Sinai, which is water poor, and only at the insistence of what they call "farmers from the north"—actually heavily armed Israeli settlers in the Demilitarised Zones (DMZs) disputed with Syria along the Upper Jordan—did the Israeli forces move three days later into the Golan. As for the attack on the West Bank, under which lies the Mountain Aquifer, in their view, it only occurred in response to Jordanian engagement. Other authors dismiss the discussion on war planning and concentrate on its hydro-strategic consequences (Naff and Matson, 1984, 57; Shapland, 1997, 17; Hillel, 1994, 161; Dolatyar and Gray, 1999, 105; Lonergan and Brooks, 1994, 124).

It would seem logical that efforts as great as those involved in war are only made if the expected results deserve it, and therefore, in 1967, several simultaneous objectives must have been in the minds of Israeli commanders. Water and land could have been a consideration, as will be seen in the following paragraphs, but also breaking the momentum that the nationalist left-leaning Arab leaderships still enjoyed at the time. As for the order of the Israeli attacks, US strategists supported the idea that the Israeli air force aimed at the Egyptians first, perhaps because Nasser was better armed and his aviation and military machine seemed a more logical target to take advantage of the surprise effect. On top of this, the entire Israeli narrative to justify launching the assault was based on the speeches delivered by the Egyptian leader. Thereafter, it would seem quite obvious that Israeli strategists hoped to wreck the

Marxist-Baath Salah Jadid leadership in Syria, which was arming and supporting the Palestinian Fedayeen since it took power in Damascus in 1966 at least as much as Nasser. In any case, it would have been absurd for the Israeli military to open two or more fronts at the same time, which would explain why they engaged first the strongest foe, Egypt, then the second strongest and most willing, Syria, and only at the end Jordan, which was under great pressure at home to come to the aid of its Arab fellows.

Some statements by Israeli officials, however, lend credibility to the argument that water was indeed an ingredient of the June War. Moshe Dayan and Ariel Sharon, both involved in planning and conducting the offensive, said that the war was fought over water and that the first shots were fired in 1965 on the Arab diversion plan (Lonergan and Brooks, 1994, 124; Bulloch and Darwish, 1993, 34). The war resulted in a radical change in the hydro-strategic position of the belligerents. Over 50% of the water resources that Israel consumes at the time of writing in 2022 come from territories occupied in June 1967. Moreover, before the war, Soviet intelligence alerted that the Israeli leadership was planning a major attack on Syria over water (see, *inter alia*, Hillel, 1994, 161; Soffer, 1999, 170). However, Israelis have later denied that water had such an important role and tended to dodge any allusion to water in discussions of the events.

3.3 The Jordan-Yarmuk water apparatus

In any case, by 1967, Israel had developed roughly all the water resources it could from rivers and aquifers, regardless of the Johnston Unified Plan, allowing it to cement its water apparatus. If Israel did fight a water war in any of these episodes, it did so between March 1965 and April 1967, when the Arabs stopped working on the Canal. Even then, however, Israeli strategists might have had several goals in mind besides water itself. As for the war of June 1967, although its results were consequential in relation to water, it clearly had much more comprehensive objectives.

The 1967 Israeli occupation of the West Bank and the Golan Heights brought several new hydro-strategic trends. From being a lower riparian country, Israel virtually became an upper riparian. With the Golan Heights, it came to control the Banias, both banks of the Upper Jordan and the entire coast of Lake Tiberias, including the Yarmuk Triangle which, as its name indicates, also includes a piece of bank of this Jordan River tributary. With the occupation of the West Bank, it also took control of the entire Mountain Aquifer. As a result, Israel has been able to block the Arab states from taking their full Johnston water allocation of Jordan-Yarmuk water. For decades, it made it difficult for Jordan to service the water uptake from the Yarmuk River into its East Ghor Main Canal. Silt and rocks accumulated at its intake, sharply reducing water flow. At the same time, Tel Aviv managed to block international loans for the building of the Syrian-Jordanian Wahda Dam at Maqarin, which would have solved the problem for Jordan of retrieving water from the Yarmuk. Israel has been able to basically ignore the Unified Plan and take a major part of the resources of the watershed. Syria sought to take its Johnston Plan water allocation by developing the resources of the Yarmuk, which in turn caused problems for Jordan. At least until the signing of the Oslo agreements in the first half of the 1990s, Israel unilaterally decided how much Mountain Aquifer water West Bank Palestinians were allowed to use and how much Jewish settlers could appropriate.

Between 1969 and 1970, the Israeli armed forces attacked and destroyed parts of the East Ghor Main Canal, claiming that the Yarmuk experienced a decreased flow, implying that the Jordanians were withdrawing more water than usual, while draught seems to have been the real culprit. Meanwhile, Israel had been pumping much more than its 25 hm^3/year Yarmuk allocation. Apparently, the actual reason for the Israeli attacks was that, in spite of the defeat of the Arab armies in the 1967 war, Palestinian guerrillas had been very active in its aftermath. Israeli leaders wanted Jordanian security to crack down on the Fedayeen. When guerrilla actions were organised from the East Bank, the Israeli army retaliated not against the militants, but against the Jordanian army and infrastructure, including water infrastructure. US mediation managed to pull an agreement between the two states, whereby the Jordanians would expel the PLO from its territory, while the Israelis would allow Jordan to rebuild the destroyed infrastructure (Naff and Matson, 1984, 45). In its effort to expel the PLO, the Jordanian army committed atrocities against Palestinians, armed and unarmed, prompting an uprising that almost ended in King Hussein losing his throne.

This is an example of an international water apparatus operating in a quite extreme and blatantly coercive way, certainly not in the sense of biopower as the administration of life. The US brokered Israeli-Jordanian agreement yielded quite meagre rewards for Jordan from the point of view of water, as did later secret "Picnic-Table Talks", Jordanian-Israeli water negotiations on the banks of the Jordan. While Israeli authors view the talks as proof of ongoing negotiation,

Jordanians feel frustrated at the lack of practical results (Lonergan and Brooks, 1994, 127–128, 141).

Events during the following decades had implications for water control in Israeli relations with Syria, Lebanon and the Palestinians. As for the Golan Heights, Syria launched, as already mentioned, a coordinated offensive with Egypt in October 1973 to try and take it back. While it managed to recover a strip of land that included the Golan provincial capital of Quneitra, the Israelis managed to keep the greater part of the territory and its most relevant water resources, that included the Banias River. Israel invaded Lebanon in 1978 under "Operation Litani", with conspicuous water apparatus undertones, and again in 1982, after which it held to the south of the country until 2000, which included the Hasbani River and sections of the Litani.

The occupation of the West Bank meant that Israel gained control over the entire Mountain Aquifer. Already before 1967, the Israelis had located a perfect area for drilling and installing powerful pumps on their side of the Green Line to extract water from the Western Slope of the Mountain Aquifer (see Map 3.1). The construction of settlements inside the West Bank implied that Israel would take even more water. This sharpened an already unequal access to water for West Bank Palestinians. As for Gazans, they suffered an even harsher situation. Israelis abstracted underground and superficial water before it reached the Gaza Strip, besides building settlements inside this territory as well (until the Ariel Sharon government dismantled them in 2005). In Chapter 4, more detailed information is given about the water situation in these territories.

3.4 Frictions along the Tigris-Euphrates: 1960–1976

During the 1960s and 1970s, Turkey, Syria and Iraq engaged in developing the water resources of the Tigris and Euphrates basin independently from each other, building their own water apparatuses. The situation was bound to cause a crisis. Given the conflicts that Syria and Iraq had among each other towards the end of the period, they not only failed to coordinate vis-à-vis the uppermost riparian, but almost had gone to war, at least apparently for water. Iran, although an upper riparian to the Tigris, showed no interest at the time in developing the waters flowing within its territory towards this watercourse and therefore was never part of negotiations either. The water conflict that it had with Iraq at the time concerned the Shatt al-Arab, where both Tigris and Euphrates join, but mostly in relation to borders and navigation rights.

Turkey, Syria and Iraq reestablished contacts after a nadir in relations in 1957–1958, immediately after the Eisenhower doctrine was formulated, and Turkey threatened to invade Syria in 1957, and Iraq in 1958. In 1960, water talks took place, but with few if any significant outcomes. The Iraqi government proposed to Turkey and Syria the coordinated development of the Tigris and Euphrates resources. The plan provided for a tri-national company to manage the rivers (Majzoub, 1994, 123–124), half of the funding for which was to come from Iraqi oil revenues and the rest from private, mostly foreign, investment (Chalabi and Majzoub, 1995, 198). Both the Turkish and Syrian Administrations rejected this proposal for the establishment of an international water apparatus in cordial terms. While Ankara had limited interest in getting into any dealings with Syria if its sovereignty over Hatay/Alexandretta was not officially recognised, Syria had unified with Egypt to form the UAR, dominated by President Nasser from Cairo, who wanted Iraq to join the Union before even considering any water development agreement. In January 1963, Syria having seceded from the Union more than a year earlier, the Iraqi government reiterated the integrated river management proposal, but it was abandoned once a coup overthrew President Abd al-Karim Qasim in February.

During the following years, Turkey and Syria independently developed large dams on the Euphrates, hardly even informing each other, and contradictions grew. Receiving very soft loans from the United States, Germany, France and Italy, as well as from the International Development Agency, the "second window" of the IBRD, and the European Investment Bank (Kenworthy, 1965), Turkey began work on the Keban Dam in 1966. The UN Food and Agriculture Organisation (FAO) and even the IBRD urged the Turkish authorities to coordinate with the downstream riparian states, but they opted to proceed alone.

The Syrian government established the Upper Euphrates Council as early as 1963, eight years after the IBRD had refused to fund the Youssef Pasha Project. Soviet advisers unsuccessfully called on Syria to coordinate its projects with Iraq, also an Eastern Bloc ally. Germany was the only Western state ready to offer loans for the reservoir that Syria was planning at Tabqa (Naff and Matson, 1984, 90). Approximately at the same time, the Arab-Israeli water conflict was heating up in relation to the Water Carrier and the Arab Canal. With Soviet aid and domestic resources, Syria began building the Tabqa reservoir in 1967 (Majzoub, 1994, 124–133) with an installed generation capacity of 824 MW and the ability to provide water to irrigate hundreds of thousands of hectares.

Contacts between Turkey, Syria, and Iraq concerning the basin continued, and sometimes included appeals for basin-wide cooperation. In 1964, the year in which Turkey sought to improve its relations with Arab countries, Turkish-Iraqi and Turkish-Syrian bilateral meetings took place. The following year, a tripartite meeting proposed establishing a joint technical committee, but the participants could not agree on its scope or if it were to become a permanent body (Kibaroğlu, 2002, 223–224).

The first water conflict on the Tigris and Euphrates basins that came close to triggering a war happened in the mid-1970s. Impounding of the two large dams built by Turkey, at Keban, and Syria, at Tabqa, began in 1974. The flow downstream to Iraq turned to a trickle. In previous years, representatives of the three countries had met several times to organise a filling schedule for the two reservoirs. Since October 1972, the delegations had agreed on the need for a joint technical commission to exchange information and seek cooperation. Although representatives of the parties made visits throughout the basin, they failed to establish mechanisms to address the concerns of the downstream countries (Kibaroğlu, 2002, 225–226).

A crisis erupted in 1975, as Baghdad sent troops to the Syrian border threatening with war unless Syria increased the flow of Euphrates water at the border. In April, Iraq called a meeting of the Arab League to protest the filling of the Tabqa Dam in Syria, which had caused the usual average Euphrates flow of 920 m³/s at the border to dwindle to a mere 197 m³/s and threatened to take whatever measures it considered necessary to resolve the situation (Naff and Matson, 1984). Damascus officials replied that they were letting flow to Iraq 71% of the water that came across the border from Turkey, which had become half of what it used to be. The League formed a technical committee involving seven Arab countries apart from the two concerned, but the Syrians withdrew in early May. Despite Soviet and Saudi mediation, the crisis rapidly deteriorated. Syria moved troops from the Israeli front to its eastern border, and rumours spread that Iraq was planning to blow up the newly built Syrian dam. Supported by the Soviets, the Saudi mediators managed to defuse the tensions by getting Syria and Iraq to agree that 60% of the water flowing down from Turkey along the Euphrates would be left to continue its course unimpeded to Iraqi territory.

According to Kolars and Mitchell (1991) and Kibaroğlu (2002, 226) a drought occurred that year, aggravating the situation and facilitating the outbreak of the conflict. For Naff and Matson (1984), the main cause of this crisis, the first to bring Tigris and Euphrates riparian states to the brink of war, was not only the drought and the impounding of the Tabqa reservoir, but also that Turkey was filling the Keban Dam.

A careful analysis of the events indicates that Saddam Hussein was actually seeking to achieve other political goals, not only a greater and more reliable water allocation. It should call our attention that the

Iraqis protested only against Damascus, without demanding Ankara to change its own dam filling schedule. This illustrates how fluid modernity had come to operate in the complex Middle East political context of the early 1970s, which should be remembered in order to make full sense of the events. Saddam Hussein, who by 1975 already had the Iraqi government well under his grip, led a faction of the Baath Party opposed to the one headed by Syrian President Hafiz al-Asad. Although both leaderships had been allied to the Soviet Union for years, and Iraq even sent troops to support the Syrian October 1973 war effort when Israel took the offensive in the Golan (Seale, 1995, 215), many things had changed by the spring of 1975. A month before the water crisis, Hussein had signed an important security and border agreement with the Shah of Iran, with the help of US Secretary of State Henry Kissinger, who promised that the United States, Iran and Israel would stop supporting the Kurdish rebellion in Iraq (Khalidi, 2009, 31, 152). Starting an antagonism with the Syrian government in those days could have pleased the US Administration and its Middle East allies.

It is worth wondering what was the real role of water itself in the crisis. Undoubtedly, the element made it possible, which suggests that it was an important cause of disagreement that could be seen as legitimate by friends and foes. However, the sequence of events and geopolitical considerations were complex and point to another quite good set of reasons for Hussein to antagonise al-Asad while leaving NATO member Turkey alone. It would seem that using the water argument allowed Hussein to show Syria his ability to wield the economic and military power of Iraq in spite of its lower-riparian position, operating on the water apparatus in coercive mode over Syria.

It would also seem that Saddam Hussein aspired to be part of the international governmental reason that the United States was leading in the Middle East. The choice of enemies, leaving Turkey aside, tends to confirm that the Iraqi government was looking to improve its contacts with the Western Bloc, so it did not address its grievances to Ankara, even though Turkey also was filling its enormous dam, carrying at least as much responsibility as Syria for the effects on Iraq. For several reasons, however, it was no easy task for Hussein to seamlessly integrate into the US-led alliance.

3.5 GAP in the governmental reason

During the 1980s, Turkey, Syria and Iraq engaged in a harsh hydropolitical contest. Turkey, determined to exploit its military, diplomatic, economic and geographical superiority, sought to continue building its water apparatus and use it to bolster both its domestic and regional governmental reason. The severest challenge was to placate a Marxist secessionist Kurdish rebellion that was rapidly expanding in the East and Southeast of the country, largely within the Tigris and Euphrates basin. Ankara wanted both Syria and Iraq to cooperate in crushing the uprising and alternated between using coercion and negotiation on water issues to achieve this goal. Syria and Iraq generally failed to coordinate among each other, but nonetheless responded, sometimes effectively. Never limiting their role to being passive recipients of Turkish mandates, Syria and Iraq resisted in various ways. As for the Kurds, all but passive, they took advantage of the contradictions and power vacuums between states that the unstable politics of the region often offered.

As will be discussed, Turkey expanded the water infrastructure plans it had in the basin, integrating them into a comprehensive Tennessee Valley Authority-inspired scheme called the Southeastern Anatolia Project (GAP). It challenges hydropolitics analysis because it really is, as official propaganda literally puts it, a multipurpose project. Much more than the averted Iraqi water war on Syria, GAP showcases the ways in which the water apparatus works. Like the large hydro-infrastructure model from which it draws inspiration, the TVA, it combines huge economic goals with various biopolitics governmentality aims. GAP features a dynamic combination of biopolitics and thanatopolitics, mainly in the domestic domain, particularly regarding Kurds, but also in the international arena, in relation to Syria and Iraq.

As soon as the Keban Dam went into operation, Turkey continued developing major works in the basin without consulting its downstream neighbours. Shortly after beginning to fill the Keban reservoir, it laid the foundation stone of the Karakaya Dam. Construction of the Atatürk Dam started in 1983, along with other projects. By 1989, all these schemes were integrated into the GAP master plan. Upon completion, the scheme would irrigate 1.7 million hectares of land and generate 27 billion kilowatt-hours of electric power annually (Ünver, 1997). It was to include 22 dams for hydropower generation or irrigation, irrigation canals, pipelines for longer distance water transfers and industrial development. Reportedly, as of 2015, eleven hydropower plants were already in operation, generating 20,174 GWh per year, and irrigating 357,000 ha (see Kankal *et al.*, 2016).

GAP and water infrastructure in East and Southeast Anatolia involve much more than hydropolitics in its restricted or even expanded understanding. They bring in a complex array of objectives that can be covered in the concept of fluid modernity. Among other things, they produce huge profits for different sorts of companies. GAP has translated and still will translate into enormous profits for construction companies. The sheer size of the infrastructural projects, although still incomplete, has already led to contracts worth tens of billions of dollars. With the expertise acquired, some of the involved companies have later gone to build dams and infrastructure abroad, even in lower Tigris-Euphrates riparian Iraq, adding to the already enormous dividends of GAP. According to the Turkish Contractors Association (cited by Akgul, 2014, 38), as the construction industry receded inside Turkey after 2000 with a drop in public and private investments in the sector, it gathered pace abroad, with dam construction contracts passing from 2.6 billion dollars in 2002 to 26.6 billion in 2012, a tenfold increase in as many years. Most of the activities took place in Turkmenistan, Russia and Iraq.

Although international banks have cashed a large part of the service of the debt incurred by the Turkish state for GAP, domestic Turkish banks also have taken part in providing financial products, especially since some international institutions have been compelled to withdraw due to the political sensitivity of the project. Grassroots, civil society and non-governmental organisations mobilised in Europe and managed to get banks to cancel loans and other financial services for GAP (Warner, 2008). Profit making, beyond that directly derived from infrastructure construction, is also important. The sales of hydro power, irrigation and agricultural implements, let alone crops, constitute further business opportunities.

The effects of infrastructure projects on water flow and quality and on the environment along the basin are severe. A PhD student in biology at Dicle University in Diyarbakir interviewed in 2013 explained that the artificial lakes created by dams transform riverine habitats into lacustrine ones, endangering the endemic biota of rivers. He had identified reduced endogenous populations of turtles and Tigris bass among other species in the Tigris, while exogenous species introduced for aquaculture projects, such as Carp, were thriving (Conde, 2016). Irrigation projects and related dams have an impact on the amount and quality of the water flow, as water is effectively abstracted and pollutants come into the stream with return flows from irrigated fields.

In Syria, after completing al-Thawra Dam at Tabqa, the state proceeded to build other hydroelectric and regulating dams on the Euphrates in 1990 and 1997 and some other irrigation and power dams on the Khabur, a tributary of the Euphrates. The scale of its projects was much smaller than GAP. In any case, Damascus has continued to honour its water commitments with Iraq.

Since the Tigris and Euphrates Rivers cross borders, or constitute them in short lengths, damming and water-use activities along their course, within GAP or otherwise, have had severe hydrological effects downstream. During the 1970s, Turkey inaugurated more dams than during the previous 50 years (Chesnot, 1993, 95). The 1980s witnessed the continuation and complication of the water conflict. Scholars have calculated that, upon completion, Turkish projects could withdraw about half of the Euphrates and Tigris discharge, and Syrian projects up to a third of the Euphrates current (see for Turkey and Syria, respectively, Kolars and Mitchell, 1991; Daoudy, 2005). Projects initiated in Iraq, although helping to alleviate the old lower Mesopotamia flooding problems and perhaps not severely impacting other countries, had an adverse effect on the local environment and on certain populations, such as those living on the once extensive marshlands of the delta. As for Turkey and Syria, many of the large dams on the Euphrates and its tributaries were for hydropower generation or discharge regulation, which consume little water, apart from evaporation. Their nuisance would be more in terms of an increase in salinity due to evaporation and the overall environmental impact of dams.

The Turkish authorities gave a political spin to the GAP from its inception, as one of its main objectives was to tackle general Kurdish disaffection and the Kurdish armed uprising that began in the early 1980s. Aiming to isolate the guerrillas from their popular base, it included several biopolitical objectives. Not only would it make jobs available in construction, agriculture and industries, all to be developed later. Flooding towns under artificial lakes would displace large portions of Kurdish rural population that often sympathised with the insurgents (see Kurdish inhabited populations in Map 3.2). As of 2000, Turkish officials had recognised that nearly 500 villages were destroyed and almost 200,000 villagers displaced (Daoudy, 2009). Planners thought, or thus they claimed, that this could allow the state to control those who remained in the countryside through irrigation schemes (Jongerden, 2010). The argument of economic growth promotion in underdeveloped Southeastern Anatolia (GAP-RDA, 2006), while perhaps real (see next paragraph), must be taken cautiously. For instance, irrigation goals, which would have made the most difference in terms of the economic well-being of the local population, are the ones to have made the least progress of overall GAP objectives. As of 2015, based on official figures, only about 20% of the expected 1.7 million ha had been developed for irrigation (see Kankal *et al.*, 2016).

Quite unsurprisingly, Kurds in Southeastern Anatolia are convinced that the GAP aims at dominating them. Interviewed in 2013,[2] mayors and municipal water officials in Diyarbakir and Batman of the pro-Kurdish Peace and Democracy Party (BDP) considered the goals of GAP to

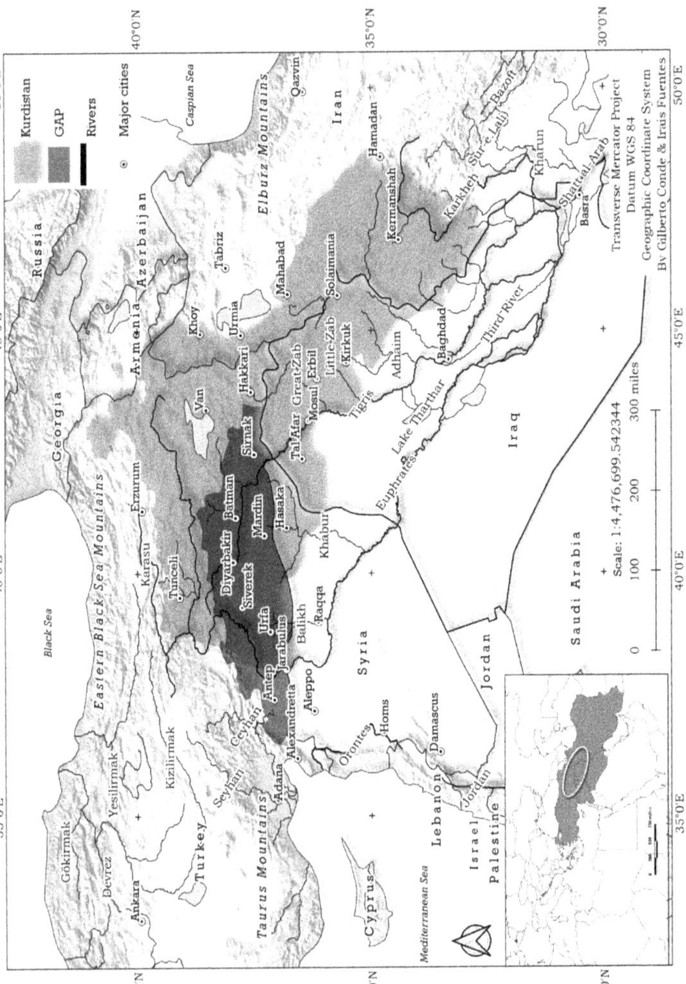

Map 3.2 Kurdish inhabited areas. Map by the author and Iraís Fuentes.

differ from those published by the General Directorate of Turkish State Hydraulic Works (DSI). Their experience tells them that the goals of the megaproject are alien to the interests of local populations.

Moreover, as much interviewed municipal officials as constituents said that GAP and other water-infrastructure schemes in the region segment their geography, wipe out their villages, disrupt settlement patterns, wreck their social fabric, change demographics by introducing Turkish population from the west of the country, shatter Kurdish historical memory by flooding archaeological sites and are designed so as to control the population and hinder the mobility of PKK activists more than for their stated purposes. All of this exacerbates the oppression of Kurds. In Dersim/Tunceli, on the banks of the Munzur River, a Euphrates tributary outside the GAP area, inhabited mainly by Kurdish and Turkish members of the minority Alevi religious group, many have a similar perception of the dams planned and being built there. Asked if Alevis opposed the construction of dams because reservoirs were to flood sacred sites, a family member interviewed on the Munzur banks told me that they opposed them not because they destroy one or many specific sacred sites, but because they destroy nature and all nature is sacred.

3.6 In the absence of governmentality: the 1980s

The last years of the 1970s and the first of the 1980s further soured the relations between Syria and both Turkey and Iraq for matters unconnected to water. Although between 1978 and 1979 the leaders of Syria and Iraq seemed to seek the unification of their two countries, the process ended up in mutual accusations of treachery (Tripp, 2002, 218–222). Simultaneously, revolution toppled the regime in Iran. When in 1980 Iran and Iraq engaged in a ravaging eight-year war, Syria was the only Arab country, together with Libya, to side with Iran, which understandably widened the rift between Syria and Iraq.

The war deepened the Iraqi reliance on Turkish trade, which, together with Syrian solidarity with Iran, hindered the possibilities of the two downstream riparian states to coordinate their opposition to Turkish damming activities. Indeed, Turkish-Iraqi bilateral trade had been rapidly growing since at least 1976, as Turkey imported large amounts of oil from Iraq while increasingly exporting back goods and services (see, for example, Engin, 1997; Elmas, 1999, 160). In 1997, a pipeline was built through Turkey to offer a Mediterranean outlet to the oil from Northern Iraq while avoiding the pre-existing conduit going through Syria (Kumral, 2016, 120–121).

Water negotiations between the parties recommenced in the early 1980s with the formation of the Joint Technical Committee. Originally, in 1980, Turkey and Iraq decided to establish the Committee alone. It started convening in 1982, and Syria joined its proceedings the following year (Majzoub, 1994, 162; Kliot, 1994, 162), meeting 16 times until 1993. Authors such as Shapland (1997, 118) assert that it had meagre results, as the Committee became little more than a forum in which delegations expressed their objectives, as its scope was never clearly defined. Nonetheless, it was within it that Turkey and Syria passed a provisional water-sharing agreement that, although later amended, still regulates sharing among the riparian states.

Also in Joint Technical Committee meetings, Turkey made what very much seems like a token proposal for the basin-wide utilisation of the Tigris-Euphrates water resources, "The three-stage plan for the optimal, reasonable use of the transboundary watercourses of the Tigris-Euphrates basin" (Turkish Republic, 1997; Kibaroğlu and Ünver, 2000). While the proposal seemed in line with the integrated management proposals of 1955, 1960 and 1964, the downstream countries had reasons to view it as a recipe for hydro-domination. The plan stresses, for example, that since the two rivers form a single basin, Iraq should use Tigris water to compensate for any shortage it might suffer on the Euphrates by using the artificial connection constructed for flood control through the Tharthar depression in northern Iraq (Turkish Republic, 1996). What the proposal fails to note is that the Tharthar depression is extremely saline and ruins, for agricultural purposes, any water passing through it and would aggravate the salinity issues that impact the lower lands of Iraq. The plan also proposed the creation of a technical commission, composed of engineers, who could assess the water resources and land in the three countries and then define the irrigation techniques to be applied, the most appropriate locations for the construction of dams, the type of crops to be planted throughout the basin, and the quantities and quality of water to be allocated to each country. Since the Turkish authorities have stated before that the climate and soils of Syria and Iraq are not the best for agriculture, one can expect the resulting proposals of Turkish engineers in any such commission.

Hydropolitical processes were gaining momentum against a backdrop of conflict amongst the three riparian countries. The biopolitical, water apparatus concerns of Turkish elites were not only related to economic interests, but also to domestic problems before, during, and after the 1980 coup and to the importance that NATO attributed to Turkey during the Cold War. Iraqi leaders, Hussein in particular, despite his relative independence from the United States and his challenge of Israel, sought to fit in the international governmental reason of Arab Gulf US allies as he was waging war with the Islamic Republic of Iran. As for Syria, which was quite isolated in the international arena, its president, Hafiz al-Asad, was considered an unrepentant Soviet ally. He had problems of his own, such as the stark opposition of the Muslim Brotherhood and other more radical fundamentalist groups, the overstretching of his security apparatus due to the intervention in Lebanon since 1978, and the Israeli intervention in this same country in 1982. Moreover, Turkey shared information with the Israelis in 1982, directly affecting the safety of the Syrian forces. Al-Asad was determined to employ every means at hand to face the challenges.

As previously argued, the Turkish government was hoping to use the Tigris and Euphrates water apparatus to tackle the Kurdish dissatisfaction. However, PKK forces had spread outside Turkey. Training camps were located in Syria-occupied Lebanon, where they prepared to launch a guerrilla movement against the Turkish state. Ankara, aware of the importance of water for Syria, exploited the subject to get Damascus to cooperate in its fight against the rebels (Jongerden, 2010). At the same time, Damascus took advantage of the linkage that Turkish authorities were making of the water and security dossiers to get a more favourable negotiation on water (Daoudy, 2005, 2009). Turkish scholars, like Güner (1998), have gone as far as stating that Syria supported the PKK partly to slow down the construction of GAP infrastructure. However, other possible goals might be more credible in explaining why the Syrian leadership decided to support the Kurdish rebellion in Turkey during the 1980s. One reason could be that it would help keeping Turkish forces busy, without forcing Syria to distract its own forces from Lebanon or the Israeli front to keep Turkey at bay. Another advantage was to limit the possibilities of having to face Kurdish dissatisfaction within its own territory, given that Syrian Kurds were getting involved in the rebellion in the northern side of the border. As for the PKK, it had its own agenda and was clearly not a simple proxy at the service of Damascus. Its relationship with the Syrian regime was one of convenience.[3] In other words, to assert that the goal of Syria in supporting the PKK was solely or even mainly to further its water agenda seems far-fetched.

In 1987, Turkey got a commitment from the Syrian leadership to stop supporting the Kurds and, in return, got a bilateral interim water agreement (Daoudy, 2005, 2009). Ankara pledged to let an average 500 m^3/s of water to flow at the Syrian border along the Euphrates. It was an interim accord because Turkey argued that it required larger amounts of water while filling up the Atatürk reservoir so, subsequently, a final settlement would have to be negotiated (Shapland, 1997, 120–121). The provisional agreement also has implications for Iraq, as its water-sharing deals with Syria depend on the amount of water that Syria gets from its upper riparian neighbour. Damascus guaranteed that no training camps were to operate inside Syria nor would guerrilla actions be allowed to be launched from its territory. The Syrian state actually forced PKK activists out of the country into Lebanon, which has no common border with Turkey, and forbid them from using Syrian territory to launch attacks (Güner, 1998). By then, however, Kurdish guerrillas were already conducting their raids into Turkey from the Qandil, a mountainous region straddling Iraq and Iran, taking advantage of the vacuum left by the war between these two countries.

The 1987 agreement seemed an important element in the water apparatus oriented towards the establishment of a regional international governmental reason. It could make the Syrian administration hope that, after the filling of Atatürk, it would be able to negotiate a greater allocation of water from Turkey. Meanwhile, Ankara expected that the decreased Syrian support for the Kurds would allow its armed forces to prevail in destroying the PKK. This was only part of a larger thanatopolitics against the Kurds that included a whole array of anti-insurgent tactics used by US allies around the world, from Indochina to Latin America, as well as using the domestic water apparatus against them. The Turkish state also seems to have calculated that the carrot of an even better water deal could allow it to get Damascus and even Baghdad implicated in crushing the Kurdish movement. In any case, nothing forced Ankara to sign the final agreement that its southeastern neighbours wanted. For Turkey, the most powerful country in the basin, fluid modernity translated into, among other things, procuring the apparently voluntary collaboration of weaker, downstream countries in its war efforts in exchange for better terms of water sharing, although still perceived as inequitable.

After a couple of years of extreme military, para-military and water apparatus efforts, Ankara considered that the PKK military capacity continued unabated and put the blame on the Syrian and Iraqi governments. Turkish authorities wanted nothing short of full Syrian and Iraqi collaboration in eliminating the insurgents. Towards the end of the 1980s, as Turkey had stopped honouring the stipulations of the bilateral Turkish-Iraqi security agreement, Hussein withdrew his country from it (Suha Bölükbaşı, cited in Kumral, 2016, 125). As for Syria, although the state had ended its support to the PKK, it stopped short of crushing it and continued giving political asylum to its leader, Abdullah Öcalan.

Inaugurating the year 1990, Ankara reverted to using water to try and coerce its lower-riparian neighbours into collaborating with its thanatopolitics towards the Kurds. Turkish authorities practically shut off the flow of the Euphrates for several weeks in January, arguing that extra water was needed to fill the Atatürk Dam, that their down-stream riparian counterparts had been informed beforehand, that its engineers had released supplementary water the previous month and would do the same in February (Turkish Republic, 1997; Kibaroğlu and Ünver, 2000). However, as the flow of the Euphrates decreased to 120 m³/s down from the agreed monthly average of 500 m³/s (Picard, 1993, 155–173), both Syria and Iraq sensed that something worse was at stake. While Syrian negotiator Waleed al-Muallem (cited by KHRP *et al.*, 2002) asserted that still in February the water flow reaching them was only 40% of what the agreement stipulated, Iraqis stated that 15% of crops where lost (Ayeb, 1998). The Turkish action, however, pushed Syria and Iraq into strengthening their bonds, at least temporarily. On April 16, in spite of frictions on other matters, the two lower riparian countries renegotiated their 1976 bilateral water deal. Syria would keep 48% of the water it received on the Euphrates and let 52% continue its course unchecked onto Iraq (Kliot, 1994; Shapland, 1997).

The highest authorities in Ankara scaled up their narrative, asserting that the Euphrates was not an international river at all, but a Turkish cross-border one. When openly declaring that the watercourse was a national Turkish river, President Turgut Özal added that his country did not have to share its resources with any other state (cited by Chalabi and Majzoub, 1995).[4]

3.7 Conclusions

If the first period of full-fledged fluid modernity already had shown the tight interaction between the global, regional, state and other scales, the 30 years going from 1960 to the end of the 1980s reaffirms it blatantly. It also confirms that the water apparatus, both domestic and inter-national, is intimately connected to the entire governmental reason, the economy and security. The third aspect that becomes apparent is the relation between the two sides of biopolitics or, in other words, between biopolitics, understood as merely the administration of life, and thanatopolitics, the administration of death.

The international governmental reason that US administrations were seeking to stabilise and even aggrandise with its Middle East allies made use of whatever means at their disposal, including of course the water apparatus. Allies were incorporated as beneficiaries, and foes were excluded even if that implied administering something different than life. The state of emergency works towards the other. It should be noted that allies in the region often had their own agendas and some-times excluded fellow members of the US alliance from water apparatus benefits, such as when the Israelis hampered the servicing of the intake to the main water canal of Jordan.

The defeat of the radical Arab nationalist camp in 1967 and even, a few years later, the rise to power of conservative elements within each state—as they took power away from the more radical currents in Egypt, Syria and Iraq—failed to produce a stable, consensual inter-national governmental reason encompassing all or even most countries in the region. Frictions continued in all fronts, even in terms of water apparatuses, along both the Jordan-Yarmuk and Mountain Aquifer basins and the Tigris and Euphrates basin.

This should not be taken as meaning that there were no agreements taking place. On the contrary, as much conflict as negotiations, agreements and even cooperation occurred during these years. Efforts were made at negotiating the terms of a governmental reason through various apparatuses, including water, through negotiations and cooper-ation. However, they often failed to work in the way the powerful hoped for.

Notes

1 An Egyptian journalist, Mohammad Hasanein Heikal was one of the closest persons to President Nasser, his confidant and ghost writer.

2 Interviews conducted by the author between May and June 2013 in Diyarbakir, Batman, Mardin, Urfa, Antep, and Tunceli/Dersim (for a more thorough discussion, see Conde, 2016).

3 Interview with Kurds in Damascus, November 2003.

4 President Özal was referring to the doctrine of absolute territorial sovereignty defended by US Attorney General Judson Harmon in a water dispute with Mexico in the 19th century (Chalabi and Majzoub, 1995, 211; McCaffrey, 1996), but which was never really followed by his country, as it could have affected its interests in relation to Mexico itself on certain watercourses or to Canada, in relation to which the United States is the lower riparian.

4 Fluid modernity in conditional mode

As might have become clear from previous chapters, fluid modernity is itself historical, and therefore takes different forms depending on the context in which it unfolds. The governmental reason itself in a domestic setup can differ quite substantially from its international equivalents, even though they are interconnected. World politics changed significantly with several developments in the 1980s and 1990s. Three of them were particularly fraught with consequences. One was the transition in world capitalism from the Keynesian to the Neoliberal economic model. The second was the end of the Cold War, with the demise of the Soviet Union and the United States becoming the sole superpower, at least for a while. The third was economic globalisation, which resulted from the combination of the first two. Although I shall not go into the details, readers should bear these phenomena in mind when thinking about fluid modernity during the period beginning in 1991.

This chapter is divided in three sections. The first and shorter one aims at establishing the general context in which politics developed in the Middle East starting 1991. The second is devoted to the fluid modernity mechanisms that have been mobilised since the beginning of Arab-Israeli talks in the context of the Madrid Process around the Jordan River and Mountain Aquifer basins. The third deals with the ups and downs of fluid modernity processes along the Tigris and Euphrates basin. During the years covered in Chapter 3, marked by fluid modernity in coercive mode, few efforts were made to build a collective governmental reason upon water apparatuses for the administration of life. In contrast, this following period, inaugurated in the early 1990s, seems more fluid, as water apparatuses appear to have been deployed on both their bio and thanatos aspects of power depending on the circumstances, which changed quite radically throughout the period.

DOI: 10.4324/9781003356905-5

4.1 The context from 1991 onwards

In the early 1990s, the administration of US President George H. W. Bush believed that it could set up a global governmental reason centred on the United States through a balancing act of coercion and consensus, which it called a "new world order" (see Bush, 1990). The Gulf crisis of that year, and the ensuing 1990 invasion of Kuwait by Iraq, allowed the United States to intervene in the region. Key to US objectives, it deserves being stressed, was not only to make most countries in the Middle East support the military campaign on Iraq, but also to promote a peaceful arrangement between Israel and its Arab neighbours under US leadership, which included fostering economic development in the Middle East (Bush, 1991). As will be seen, this idea included developing the fluid-modernity water apparatus. Although the succeeding administration of Bill Clinton focused on economic issues, it continued many policies inherited from its predecessor.

With the new century, the administration of George W. Bush, inaugurated in January 2001, sought, especially after the September 11 attacks on the United States, to shift the strategy from one centred on the governmental reason—which in its logic "squandered" the opportunities that the "uni-polar moment" gave to the United States—to one based on domination, coercion and repression. In more Gramscian terms, the new strategy was to move away from hegemony towards Empire (see *inter alia* Hobsbawm, 2008). The United States militarily occupied Iraq for a prolonged period of time, intervened openly in a broadly redefined Middle East and stepped up its pro-Israeli bias, all of which contributed to make instability the face of the new *status quo* in the region. This context brought renewed difficulties to certain states, and in general to populations, particularly to Palestinians in the early 2000s. In terms of fluid modernity, Israel moved away from developing the more consensual aspects of the water apparatus.

It should be mentioned that relations among other states in the region did improve, at least for a time in the early 2000s. Some, namely Turkey and Syria, and Syria and Jordan, resorted to several dispositifs, including the water apparatus, to lubricate their better relations and, *vice versa*, build on the latter to strengthen their water apparatus. The Turkish-Syrian rapprochement seemed to inch towards the establishment of a regional governmental reason, although one in which some, especially Kurdish, populations, were sacrificed, excluded as part of a state of emergency.

After the breakdown of the US imperial model around 2006, US administrations have hesitated between seeking to re-establish a governmental reason, to take distance from Middle-East affairs, or outright impose their will. Turmoil and an important degree of chaos have afflicted the region. Since December 2010, with the spread of the Arab Spring uprisings, populations have taken centre stage. Repression of the social movements and the breaking out of war in Syria, not to mention other countries, deepened the instability. At least for the time being, a lack of formal agreements in general, also concerning water, has become the permanent status. New centres of international governmental reason have appeared. They have included most elites but excluded many populations. Fluid modernity, however, has all but gone away. Taking new forms, rebels and social movements have also worked on water apparatuses.

4.2 Water and Arab-Israeli negotiations

Once the US-led forces declared the Gulf War over in late February 1991, the United States launched an Arab-Israeli negotiations scheme, kick-started at the Madrid Conference for Peace in the Middle East. US administrations put pressure on the sides to meet, negotiate, discuss peace and even reach some agreements. As in the 1950s, both Madrid and Oslo had an important fluid modernity aspect, although without being *the* core of the process. The possibility of reaching agreements around water was used to lure regional leaders into negotiating, while water also came to be considered a requisite for peace. As will be seen, progress was made in water negotiations in several tracks. Eventually, however, the Madrid and Oslo processes were interrupted, hampering the prospects for comprehensive long-term Arab-Israeli peace, particularly for Palestinians, while the water conflict has deepened.

Inaugurated on 30 October 1991, the Madrid Conference brought together for three days delegations from Israel, Jordan, Lebanon, Syria and the Palestinians. Organised along two tracks, the bilateral one sought to gather each of the Arab sides with Israel at a separate negotiating table to discuss the terms of an eventual peace agreement. In each, water figured high in the agenda. Simultaneously, the so-called multilateral track was organised in five different fora around subjects deemed to improve the negotiating environment. Many states, not only the directly concerned ones, along with prospective funding parties from other countries and international financial institutions could participate in these groups, attuned to the rampant neoliberal ideology of the times. Water and its management were one of the five subjects to be discussed. It should be mentioned that both the Syrian and Lebanese delegations abstained from participating in these and the other multilateral gatherings, arguing that nothing could come out of them as long as just and durable peace agreements were not signed.

Turkey, presenting itself as a fluid-rich country by regional standards, sent a delegation to the water multilateral talks with a bold though questioned proposal. Özal declared that his country was ready to build a "Peace Pipeline" to convey and sell water to Middle East countries. Seeking to placate Arab concerns, Turkish leaders declared that the project was not conceived to sell water to Israel and that the water they wanted to market would not come from the Tigris or Euphrates Rivers, but from the Seyhan and Ceyhan, which flow entirely within Turkish borders. Immediately, Israeli experts started to study the ways in which Turkish water transfers to neighbouring states could alleviate water stress in their country. If for instance the Kingdom of Jordan received substantial volumes, more Jordan River water could be freed for use in Israel (Kally, 1993, 18; Wolf, 1995, 16). As soon as June 1991, Syrian officials expressed their objections, given that they and Iraq had an outstanding water conflict with Turkey. Other Arab countries also criticised the scheme (Starr, 1995, 115). Even if the water was to come from the Seyhan and Ceyhan Rivers, Arab representatives were reluctant to depend on Turkey for their water. It should be said that in those years Arab opinion was extremely sensitive about Turkish readiness to use water as a weapon, as it seemingly did in January of the previous year when it brought the flow of the Euphrates River to an almost complete halt (see Chapter 3). Later, other ideas were made public, such as the already mentioned scheme of transferring water from Turkey to Israel by sea, in Medusa Bags or tankers, which would allow circumventing Syria.

Since the more substantial water issues were dealt with in bilateral negotiations, the water multilateral track had few practical results. Nonetheless, it represented an innovative fluid modernity mechanism designed to bolster the water apparatus. Increased contacts took place between water experts from Jordan, Palestine and Israel in the water working forum in efforts designed to form a water epistemic community. The US National Research Council led a panel of experts from the three parties that produced a book summarising the water situation in the Jordan-Yarmuk and Mountain Aquifer basins, as well as the state of the art in water saving technology and methods to improve consumption efficiency (CSWSME, 1999).

4.2.1 The Israeli water apparatus on the Palestinians

As argued in Chapter 1, it makes little sense to disconnect fluid-modernity phenomena between scales, the global, regional and sub-regional, the domestic and the colonial, not to mention other more subtle ones, as if scales were neatly cut themselves. It would be similarly absurd to pretend that nothing changes between scales and through time, so "fluid" is a very apt adjective for this reason as well.

Needless to say, the way Israel deals with Arab states differs quit substantially from how it treats the Palestinians, although it enjoys a position of power in all these cases. Through the decades, it has used its diplomatic, military and economic resources to take more water from all possible sources, surface or underground, or even non-conventional ones. It has resorted to more coercive methods sometimes and to more consensual ones in others, but the result always has been an asymmetrical relationship, and of course, the asymmetry is greater with the Palestinians. Israeli nationals, whether in Israel or in the settlements colonising territories occupied in 1967, systematically enjoy a greater average annual allocation of water than Palestinians.

As is widely known, Palestinian-Israeli negotiations culminated in the 1993 and 1995 Interim Oslo Accords, while permanent-status negotiations, originally set to begin no later than 4 May 1996, were expected to lead to a comprehensive peace deal by 1999, which was meant to include issues of "common interest", including water, alongside statehood, borders, Jerusalem, refugees, Israeli settlements. Almost three decades after Oslo, however, no successful permanent-status negotiations have taken place nor seem forthcoming. Oslo led to the establishment of an autonomous Palestinian authority to administer the most densely populated areas of the Israel occupied territories of the West Bank and Gaza, but it comes second to effective Israeli control.

The Oslo accords failed to tackle, let alone solve, the situation of dire water stress under which the Palestinians lived. Under the 1993 Declaration of Principles on Interim Self-Government Arrangements (Oslo I) the question of water was not really considered. The Gaza/Jericho Agreement of May 1994 provided limited water control to a Palestinian Water Authority. The September 1995 Agreement (Oslo II) dealt more extensively with the fluid. Israel recognised that Palestinians had water rights. Transfers in a first stage included 28 hm³/y from the Eastern slope of the Mountain Aquifer to the West Bank and 5 hm³/y to the Gaza Strip, which later were to increase to between 70 and 80 hm³/y, but this has not materialised (Kliot, 2000, 191–217). The parties also agreed it was key to secure water imports from third countries and accepted the principle of water markets to allow the two entities to trade in water when deemed convenient.

Under the guise of equality, the agreements actually reflected the asymmetry of power between the State of Israel and the Palestinian

Authority. True, the 1995 deal gave the Palestinians some extra water and provided for an Israeli-Palestinian Water Committee to coordinate water management in the West Bank during the interim period (Shapland, 1997, 31–35). However, it also established a joint water police, which prevented Palestinians from drilling new wells, unless authorised by the joint committee (Wolf, 2000, 106–107). The establishment of the committee implied that Israeli authorities had veto power over decisions concerning water management in the West Bank and Gaza, while no similar power was given to the Palestinian Water Authority concerning Israeli settler water use in the West Bank and Gaza, let alone in Israel proper.

Different formulae were proposed to calculate the part of Mountain Aquifer water that legally corresponded to each party. Israeli negotiators and scholars argued that Israelis were entitled to the lion's share, since they were the first to develop and make use of it. They asserted that this was the case already before 1967 (Wolf, 1994, 32; Wolf, 1995, 61–62; Shuval, 1996, 145–146). Such arguments are based on one set of principles of water law, *absolute territorial integrity*, that privileges established rights, rather than a balance of different legal principles. Already making progress in the codification of international water law in the mid-1990s, the UN International Law Commission sought to weigh all legal considerations, including acquired rights, but a similar weight was given to planned uses. As mentioned in Chapter 1, in 1997, the United Nations approved a Water Law Convention based on these balanced principles (McCaffrey, 2001), and Israel abstained, but did not vote against it (see Rieu-Clarke *et al.*, 2012).

Fluid modernity under occupation has produced a type of biopolitics in which water benefits also are distributed to the occupied, but scarcely. An equitable formula that limited significant harm, in keeping with the Convention, would have allotted Palestinians a quite substantial share of Mountain Aquifer waters and would have required Israel to share fresh water with Gaza. Already in the early 1990s, with a much greater confusion as to what constituted customary international law than there is today, Palestinian scholars concluded that the West Bank was legally entitled to at least 25% of the water from the aquifer to allow self-sufficiency through appropriate water resources management techniques, even without international water transfers (Zarour and Isaac, quoted in Lonergan and Brooks, 1994, 130, 133). Although the percentage according to the Treaty Law can be assessed, and would give Palestinians a substantially greater allocation, the Israelis, to justify the inequitable distribution, have tilted their water discourse towards needs and away from rights (Zeitoun, 2011, 77–79).

While Israelis consume an average of 1750 hm³/y for agricultural, industrial and household uses, Palestinians only have access to roughly 300 hm³/y, about a sixth of what Israelis get. When looking at consumption per inhabitant, the situation is not much fairer, as in 2003 each Israeli was consuming an average of 753 litres per day, and a Palestinian 260 litres per day, or roughly one third (Zeitoun, 2011, 127–136), and this was only after the Oslo II accords had been implemented for almost a decade. Israel has been exploiting the fresh water Western Aquifer (Western slope of the Mountain Aquifer) by using powerful pumps. Israel withdraws 340 hm³/y, while Palestinians get 22 hm³/y from this source, considered the best groundwater source in the territory. Taking only the West Bank into account, it should be kept in mind that Israelis have established settlements there since the war of 1967. In 2003, 2.4 million Palestinians and 230,000 Israeli settlers, less than a tenth, lived there. However, the settlers were getting slightly more than a quarter of all the water being consumed in the West Bank.

The water situation for Palestinians in the Gaza Strip is much worse than in the West Bank. Israelis abstract the water from Wadi Gaza (a seasonal river) that used to flow from the West Bank to Gaza. Although the Aquifer under Gaza is part of the Coastal Aquifer that runs along the Mediterranean Coast of Israel, nothing was said in the Oslo II Accord about Palestinian water rights from this source. While the aquifer has an estimated recharge rate of 485 hm³/y, Israelis pump out almost 430 hm³/y, which leaves only 55 hm³/y for Gazans. But the over 2 million inhabitants of the Strip cannot get along with less than 130 hm³/y. The over exploitation of the Aquifer has made its water brackish, as sea water has infiltrated it due to the water pressure difference, with chloride levels exceeding 400 ppm. (The US Environmental Protection Agency standard is 250 ppm.) The US Agency for International Development (USAID) had planned to build a desalination plant in Gaza, but all Agency programs for the area were interrupted when Hamas won the elections in 2006 (Zeitoun, 2011, 46–48, 185).

As decades have passed and a permanent status agreement has not materialised, the interim accords *de facto* have become permanent, crystallising the terms of the hierarchical relationship. Palestinians have been condemned to gradually deteriorating conditions and expensive access to water. For Mark Zeitoun (2011, 150), the terms of the accords marked the transition from "empire", in which Israel imposed its water decisions by force on the Palestinians, to hegemony, where force is combined with consent in defining the negotiated terms of asymmetrical power. The bilateral water cooperation has become little more than one of the forms taken by the conflict (Selby, 2003; Zeitoun, 2011).

Palestinian leaders could argue in their discharge that they signed disadvantageous terms because they had believed that very soon permanent status negotiations were to be held, in which they hoped to obtain better terms. Since they never really took place, the interim accords became permanent as well as their unfair water provisions. It is almost certain, however, that even permanent status negotiations would have led to unfair terms. Thus, Palestinians find themselves in a position in which they can only demand an increased share of water through protests, but other more pressing demands usually lie at the core of mobilisations.

In 2000, before leaving office, President Bill Clinton made a last-ditch effort to save the moribund Palestinian-Israeli negotiations by brokering a permanent deal, but failed. Israeli Prime Minister Ehud Barak made an offer that fell short of Palestinian self-determination as he presented a map of a Palestinian state in much less than the territory that Israel captured in 1967 and fragmented into a large number of virtually disconnected territories bordering no state other than Israel. This generated an understandably deep feeling of frustration among Palestinians, who had placed their hopes on what they had thought was a peace process.

In that context, Ariel Sharon made the open provocation of walking, guarded by hundreds of security personnel, through the al-Haram al-Sharif and al-Aqsa Compound, in Jerusalem, which is the third holiest site of Muslims in the world, and a sign of pride for Palestinians. Protests immediately started, which were confronted violently by Israeli forces, killing and wounding many Palestinians. A new Intifada began. Among other actions, in late 2000 and early 2001, Israeli military and settlers took Palestinian civil water facilities as military targets in the West Bank. They also filled wells with sand, sniped Palestinian farmers, destroyed agricultural land and uprooted olive trees (for Western sources, see Derfner, 2001, 29; and Foundation for Middle East Peace, 2001).

Shortly after, Sharon took office as Prime Minister of Israel and George W. Bush as President of the United States. An already dire situation deteriorated even more after September 2001. In March 2002, Israel launched a military operation that Jan Selby (2003, 2–3) considers the real end of the Oslo process. He recounts a number of military actions that on top of violating human rights, targeting Palestinian civil institutions and destroying a great amount of infrastructure, aimed at the fledgling Palestinian water apparatus. "As with every other area of Palestinian life, water supply services were gravely affected", Selby writes. The Israeli forces destroyed water infrastructure, killed or arrested water engineers, and piped water services were interrupted. The West Bank and Gaza were put in a state of siege.

That same year, Israel began to build a barrier, which has actually segregated West Bank Palestinians. Although Israeli leaders call it a "fence", the barrier is formed in parts by a cement wall, and in others by a 50-to-70-m-wide strip, flanked by two parallel 1.8-m tall razor-wire triangular-profile fences, deep trenches, a 9-m-tall fence, a military road and a number of other physical obstacles and sophisticated electronic security technology. Regardless of its relative effectiveness in protecting Israeli citizens (Novosseloff and Neisse, 2007), detailed observation of the barrier layout tends to confirm that other concerns have been taken into consideration in its planning. The system lies entirely within the West Bank side of the Green Line, which delineates the international border of Israel until before the start of the 1967 war.[1] Since its path more or less follows the permanent status borders that Israelis have proposed in several occasions, Palestinians feared that Israeli leaders sought to turn the barrier into the *de facto* border between Israel and a future Palestinian entity and leave an important part of the drilling area of the Western Aquifer outside their territory. According to Zeitoun (2011, 93–98, 159), however, although the barrier does undercut the access of a number of farmers and town dwellers to land and water, this is not its underlying rationale.

Given that occupation has become the permanent status—a state of emergency turned into the rule—with differentiated rights according to the ethnic/religious background of the populations living under its authority, many have concluded that Israel has effectively become an Apartheid state or at least commits the crime of Apartheid on West Bank and Gaza Palestinians. Although he later apologised for using the term, in April 2014, then US Secretary of State John Kerry warned that Israel risked becoming an Apartheid state if it persisted in occupying the West Bank and Gaza (Beaumont, 2014). Seven years later, Human Rights Watch (2021) published a study that found that Israel was committing the crimes of Apartheid on the Palestinians of the West Bank and Gaza. The following year, Amnesty International (2022) concluded that Israel makes Palestinians live under a system of Apartheid, which constitutes a crime against humanity. The two reports concluded that Palestinians are systematically discriminated against in relation to many issues, including water.

In terms of fluid modernity, biopolitics and the governmental reason, what becomes apparent is that the interconnected water apparatus in Israel/Palestine administers life for one part of the population—for Jewish Israelis, who are considered full nationals, whether born in Israel or not—but much less so for Palestinians. They live in spaces of exception, under an accord dubbed "interim", giving them a restricted right to water, often brackish water. The water and security apparatusses overlap. Both are constitutive of the governmental reason that helps keep Palestinians under control. The state of emergency, paraphrasing again Walter Benjamin (1989), is not the exception but the rule.

4.2.2 *Water and Jordanian-Israeli peace*

Taking advantage of the negotiating spree of the early 1990s, once the Oslo process made headway, the Kingdom of Jordan and Israel signed a peace treaty on 26 October 1994, which included an extensive annex on water. According to Soffer (1999, 176), the fluid was as difficult to negotiate as borders. The Johnston Plan was the untold basis of the water deal, although representatives failed to address the 100 hm³/y of upper Jordan River waters that the Unified Plan allocated to the Kingdom. Curiously, the 1955 scheme came through as the most authorised framework for interstate water sharing. The terms of the 1994 annex seem relatively favourable to Jordan, but its ambiguous wording has allowed Israel to dodge some of its stipulations (Fischhendler, 2008). The situation in Jordan has worsened since 2011, as a steep increase in population occurred due to the inflow of Syrian refugees fleeing from repression and war, boosting water demand in one of the most parched countries in the world (Talozi *et al.*, 2019).

The agreement offered the provisions of a common Israeli-Jordanian water apparatus. Israeli negotiators agreed to limit their Yarmuk withdrawals to a ceiling of 25 hm³/y, while the Jordanians agreed to store an extra 20 hm³/y of Yarmuk winter waters in Lake Tiberias, to be returned to them in the summer, which could help reduce salinity in the main surface water reservoir of Israel (Shapland, 1997, 28–29; Soffer, 1999, 186). Tel Aviv also committed to give desalinated brackish water from the lower Jordan, offer assistance in desalinating 50 hm³/y, assist in the uptake of Yarmuk water into the East Ghor Canal, cooperate in increasing the quality of Lower Jordan River water and consider participating in other water projects. Implementation, however, has been complicated, to say the least. Amman had to break diplomatic contacts in the 1990s before Israel actually let go half of the above-mentioned water (Soffer, 1999, 182). Since the signing of the agreement in 1994, the Israeli side has failed to build the desalination plant that would have allowed for the delivery of the other 25 hm³/y to Jordan (Haddadin, 2011; Talozi *et al.*, 2019). Only in 2021 did the parties reach agreements that should get the desalinated water flowing into Jordan (Staff, 2021).

Meanwhile, Syrian-Jordanian water relations improved for some years after 2000. The Jordanians had complained for decades that while the Israelis prevented them from abstracting Yarmuk water, the Syrians were taking water from this watercourse far beyond their Johnston-Plan allocations. In the early 2000s, however, Syrians and Jordanians managed to make some progress in negotiations in the context of a general improvement in their relationship. Syrians aided the Jordanians to install pumps on the Yarmuk, which allowed Jordan to withdraw a larger share of water. Between 2003 and 2004, they began working on the al-Wahda Dam at Maqarin, finally completed in 2011. Although water quality problems followed (Al-Taani, 2013), and the flow of the Yarmuk downstream from Syria seems to have decreased, the dam represented a big boon for access to water in Jordan, as it became one of its two largest water reservoirs. Certainly, any steps previously made toward a bilateral governmental reason, on the basis of the water apparatus among others, have been unmade in the context of the war that has ravaged Syria after 2011.

4.2.3 Water in Syrian-Israeli negotiations

Towards the end of 1995, Syrian-Israeli peace seemed to be in reach. The murder of Prime Minister Yitzhak Rabin by an Israeli extremist frustrated it, however, and an agreement remains elusive. The representatives of Rabin and Hafiz al-Asad had worked out the details of the peace treaty. Water, along with security concerns, was at the core of negotiations (Cobban, 1999). The fluid has always been a core topic in the agenda, but, rather than the water dispositif, the real obstacles seem to lie more in the security apparatus and in Israeli domestic governmentality concerns.

The Syrian leadership made it clear, from the beginning, that it wanted to steer clear of participating in what can be understood as a bi-national governmental reason. They even declared that they might be ready to accept fuller cooperation with time, building on smaller steps. The Israeli side appeared not to disagree. The two main objectives of the Syrian Administration were to recover the entire Syrian territory lost in 1967, or almost, and fix mutually recognised borders with Israel. As for Israeli goals, they centred on onouring full recognition and normal relations once and for all, which also had implications vis-à-vis Lebanon and its border with Israel, ensuring continued and unchecked access to the water that they had been abstracting from the Golan Heights, guaranteeing its quality, and excluding direct Syrian contact with Lake Tiberias (for more on the Israeli position, see Hof, 2000, 150–167). However, it seems clear that Rabin and later Israeli prime ministers have been mostly interested in the security aspects of an eventual deal with Syria.

On several occasions, Israeli leaders used water as an argument to refuse signing a peace treaty with Syria or to make progress in negotiations. In 1996, Shimon Peres and Ehud Barak said that land was negotiable, but not water (cited by Wolf, 2000, 108). In 2000, then-Israeli Prime Minister Ehud Barak refused to withdraw to the limits that Rabin had set five years earlier, although they implied making gains in relation to the pre-June 1967 border. In spite of making headway in the negotiations, Barak later decided to sit on the process and eventually abandoned it. The argument centred on hydro-strategic concerns. The Syrians had accepted most of the political and security demands, although asserting that normalisation could only be built upon a practice of good relations. They accepted the initial territorial demands and virtually all the water ones. The Israelis sought to keep a strip of land along the Golan bank of Lake Tiberias and the Syrians agreed. They also committed not to touch the water flowing into the lake or passing through the Golan and discharging into the Jordan River. The main difference related to the width of the strip off Tiberias (see the account by US negotiator Dennis Ross, 2011).

After the collapse of negotiations in 2000 and the already mentioned arrival of conservative administrations to office in both Israel and the United States, the Syrian-Israeli process came to a standstill. It was only after the 2006 war on Lebanon that Israeli leaders started considering re-activating talks with Syria, even though the Syrian Administration had made several advances before and after the US invasion of Iraq in 2003. Sharon systematically refused to consider them, arguing that the Syrians had to come to the negotiating table without conditions, hinting that he rejected the progress made in previous talks. In one occasion, Sharon told the Israeli press that the benefits of peace with the Syrians were less than the costs and complained that peace with Syria would imply forgoing the Golan Heights (Alon, 2004).

Later in the decade, new efforts were made. Turkish mediation made some headway during both the Bush and Barack Obama administrations, but came to a dead end as Israel attacked the Gaza strip in late 2008 (Conde, 2013, 191–194). In the following years, the United States made secret efforts to broker a deal. The second Benjamin Netanyahu administration demanded that Syria cut all ties to Iran, Hezbollah and other parties that Israel considered its archenemies. The Bashar al-Asad administration agreed to this on condition of returning to the

4 June 1967 green line, while Syria would recognise full Israeli sovereignty over Lake Tiberias. Although the Israelis agreed to the principle of returning to the old armistice line, its exact location was disputed, particularly concerning the western bank of the Upper Jordan River (Hof, 2022). Talks seemed promising, but then everything changed. As mass demonstrations filled the Syrian streets in the context of the Arab Spring, Asad chose to violently crack down on the protesters, which soon led to an all-out war inside Syria. The US Administration, and maybe the other party as well, lost interest in the negotiation process. No new openings seem to have taken place since then.

4.2.4 Water in the Lebanese-Israeli file

For several reasons, Lebanon and Israel made little if any progress in negotiations in the 1990s. The Israeli occupation of South Lebanon from 1982 until 2000 led to a permanent state of violence that made peace particularly difficult to achieve. The Lebanese Civil War only started to recede after the signing of the 1989 Taif Accords, even though unrest continued over the Syrian presence in the country, which only ended in 2005. Through those years, Damascus played a heavy role in defining Lebanese foreign policy. In the 1990s, it was clear that a breakthrough in Lebanese-Israeli negotiation was contingent on Syrian-Israeli peace, which, as seen, failed to take place.

Lebanese objectives went beyond the Israeli evacuation of occupied territories and included at least a commitment to fixed borders. For the Israeli state, the Lebanese border is of high concern. All major Israeli operations inside Lebanon have proven extremely hazardous and politically costly (Murden, 2000). Hezbollah, the Lebanese resistance movement linked to Iran but also to Syria, has proven able and disciplined and has managed to attract domestic respect (Norton, 2000). During 2000, Hezbollah increased its attacks on the occupying forces, and Israel chose to withdraw unconditionally from Southern Lebanon. By "unconditionally", it meant without signing a peace deal, i.e., not heeding Lebanese and Syrian demands and taking a card from Syrian diplomatic hands. But it also meant creating new strategic concerns. Six years later, Israeli armed forces tried to reoccupy the region but had to retreat south of the border after only one month of launching the operation (Achcar and Warschawski, 2006).

In relation to water, the bilateral agenda was marred with suspicions concerning Israeli intentions over the water resources of south Lebanon. These apprehensions go back to the Zionist proposals at the 1919 Versailles Peace Conference mentioned in Chapter 2, which asked to set the border of Palestine so as to leave the lower Litani River inside the territory that they planned to transform into the Jewish state. In the late 20th century, rumours inside Lebanon claimed that the Israeli occupation actually aimed at withdrawing water from the Litani and blocking the Lebanese from using fluid from the Wazzani Springs (*inter alia*, Amery, 2000; Wolf, 2000).

The unilateral Israeli withdrawal from south Lebanon in 2000 confirmed that there was no "water imperative" for Israel to retain any of this territory simply for its water-related importance (Wolf, 2000, 63–120). It also lifted worries about alleged Israeli water abstractions from the Litani, although some continued asserting that the tight security maintained by the Israeli military over the elbow of the river during the occupation apparently was used by Israeli water experts to make studies concerning the viability of diverting part of its flow into the Upper Jordan (Amery, 2000, 121–149). The fact remains, nonetheless, that the Israelis abstained from making any diversion there.

This being true, Israeli officials undoubtedly allocate a strategic importance to the flows from the Wazzani Springs and the Hasbani River. They have repeatedly shown their readiness to flex military and diplomatic muscle to prevent Lebanon from withdrawing even its Johnston allocation from these sources. With the 1978 occupation, the Israeli military gained control of the Wazzani Springs and, according to Western reports, they used the pro-Israeli South Lebanon Army (SLA) militia to stop Lebanese villagers from drilling wells in the area. Thus, the Israeli authorities ensured that a large part of the 35 hm³/y Johnston allocation to Lebanon from the Hasbani flowed freely into Israel (Naff and Matson, 1984, 49–50). Wolf (1995, 57–59; 2000, 91–93) rebutted these assertions, but limited his evidence to quoting an Israeli military source testifying to a supposed land and water nationalism of SLA leader Saad Haddad. Hussayn Amery (2000, 121–149) has correctly criticised the reliance of this argument on Israeli military sources.

Post-occupation Israeli practice has shown that water in Lebanon is still an important concern for Israeli strategists. A conflict over the Wazzani Springs broke out in the second half of 2002, as the Lebanese government sought to improve standards of living in the south and stem the local economy after the withdrawal of Israeli occupation forces by developing local water resources within Johnston allocations. Pumps and pipelines were laid to withdraw 3.6 hm³/y of Wazzani water for drinking and urban use in 40 villages, in addition to 7 hm³/y already being withdrawn with a pump installed the year before to service several towns in the area. Although one could speculate that this amount might increase in the future for irrigation purposes in South Lebanon, it would have been unfeasible at least while land mines from occupation times remained in place (Jansen, 2002). Israeli forces already had installed a pipeline then to water the town of Gajar, which straddles Lebanon and the Israeli occupied Golan. However, the rest of the area remained dry for decades.

The Israelis forced the Lebanese to stop developing the Wazzani waters. Sharon threatened to take action against the new facilities if inaugurated, claiming that an "understanding" already existed. The Israeli press ran articles stating that the Arabs had never ratified the Johnston Plan, implying that as long as no formal agreement existed, Israel was to maintain the fluid *status quo* (Benziman, 2002), which meant keeping almost the entire current of the upper Jordan tributaries to flow unchecked into Israel, as had been the case since the shelling of the Arab diversion works in 1965 and the occupation of the Golan in 1967.

Tel Aviv also used the symbolic role of water during its 2006 military campaign in Lebanon. The fluid was not at the core of the war, but its water apparatus value was used to add to the psychological pressure on the Lebanese. In its failed 33-day war effort to crush Hezbollah, Israeli sources stated that their goal was to occupy Lebanon up to the Litani River. This was asserted not only through Israeli media, but also in 17 million flyers in Arabic dropped by Israeli planes over towns south of the Litani, in which they warned the Lebanese to go northwards or face being considered an enemy combatant force (Friedman, 2006). It was a multi-pronged frame. Not only those who remained could be killed or arrested as enemy fighters, it implied that Israel sought to reoccupy the South but free of its population, suggesting they could seek to remain there indefinitely, as done before with Palestinian and Syrian occupied territories. Moreover, mentioning the Litani could be expected to invoke fluid modernity ideas connected to the strategic importance of water in the region and the above mentioned 1919 Zionist request to get the area. Although the combined frame seems to have had mostly psychological-war aims, it is noteworthy that water was an element of the whole, as ideas on the importance of the fluid had been established through contemporary history and now were being mobilised to scare the Lebanese.

4.3 A Tigris-Euphrates water apparatus

After the end of the Cold War, Turkish leaders have sought to mobilise the water apparatus in various ways, in terms of biopolitics as administration of life and its opposite, both within its borders and across. In relation to Syria and Iraq, it has oscillated between cutting the flow of rivers to offering diplomatic advances for a regional governmental reason. Turkish authorities also held a shifting policy between these two extremes in relation to Kurds in the East and Southeast of the country. Many things changed in 1990, as Washington reassessed its global strategy once the Soviet Bloc crumbled after 1988 and brought the Middle East to centre stage. US regional allies sought to prove their usefulness, and water came again to be valued as an apparatus of international governmental reason. The 1990 Gulf crisis and the subsequent War on Iraq by a world coalition led by the United States offered Turkey an opportunity to reiterate its allegiance, and Syria, a former Soviet ally, to vow its goodwill. The war itself and the post-war US and UK intervention in Iraq fragmented space in new ways, producing new crucial contradictions. Sanctions and the declaration of a no-fly zone over the north of Iraq not only led to the formation of a *de facto* Kurdish autonomous region there, it also allowed for the consolidation of a space from which Kurdistan Workers' Party (PKK) guerrillas could continue their armed struggle. The Turkish military felt powerless and hoped to get Syria and Iraq to collaborate in their efforts against the revolutionary group.

4.3.1 The Tigris-Euphrates apparatus in the 1990s

During part of the 1990s, Turkish foreign policy continued to utilise water as a means to entice or coerce its southeastern neighbours into collaborating with its domestic security concerns. It did so under the guise of negotiations within the context of the tripartite Joint Water Committee, which continued to convene for a few more years until 1993. Ankara and Damascus sought a new rapprochement in that framework, in which the Turkish authorities tried to convince Hafiz al-Asad to help with suppressing the Kurds in exchange for a larger water allocation. In 1992, the two countries signed a new security protocol. Syria stated that the PKK was not legal in Syria, that it would fight terrorism and that Turkey should discuss the PKK question with Lebanon, as training camps were located in the Beqaa Valley, not in Syria (al-Jahmani and Ousy, 1999, 55–56; Daoudy, 2009). Turkish authorities continued waving the water carrot for some time. The Özal Administration sought to take advantage of the new post-Cold War and post-Gulf War context, in which the Syrian government had sided with the Bush senior administration and took part in the Madrid Middle East Peace Conference.

After Özal died in April 1993, Soleyman Demirel left the premiership to become President and Tansu Çiler, widely seen as pro-United States, was sworn in as Prime Minister. The new administration, changed course, abandoning the Joint Technical Committee, which was not to convene again for almost 15 years. Even though Syria and Iraq were still at odds with each other, they continued to harmonise their hydro diplomacy. Turkey made a series of proposals, mainly aimed at justifying its position and its mega-projects to world public opinion and international banks, given that, as mentioned in Chapter 3, the denunciations made by Damascus, Baghdad, the Kurds and even some European NGOs were having a wide echo (Warner, 2004).

The Turkish political situation was very fluid, and Syria was in the middle of debates. While Damascus had engaged in negotiations with Israel for the previous three years, Turkey had strengthened its ties with this country. Simultaneously, the PKK was reinforcing its activities, and the Islamist opposition Refah (Welfare) Party was gaining ground among the Turkish electorate and even managed to receive the largest number of votes in the general elections of December 1995, though it failed to build a large enough parliamentary alliance to form a government. In February, the Turkish military high command passed a strategic agreement with its Israeli counterparts, which was made public by the Turkish side two months later (Robins, 1997).

Politicians in Turkey began a fluid modernity debate. On the one hand, Prime Minister Mesut Yılmaz sought to rouse the nationalist sentiments of Turks by asserting that Turkey would not relinquish a drop of its water to Syria and Iraq (al-Jahmani and Ousy, 1999, 62). On the other, Necmettin Erbakan, the leader of Refah, appealing to feelings of Muslim solidarity, said that the water issue was one of the problems that the West had sown among Turks, Arabs and Muslims, just like the problems of borders and minorities, seeking to spoil forever the relations between Islamic countries (al-Jahmani and Ousy, 1999, 66). In late June, for several political circumstances, Yılmaz had to resign, and Erbakan took office as Prime Minister in coalition with Çiler, who became Minister of Foreign Affairs, perhaps to relieve allies in the United States and Israel as well as the military establishment. Erbakan wanted to mend fences with Syria, but had a narrow margin of action. The military made clear to him as soon as he took office that they would not allow him to change course on Middle East policy (Altunisik, 2000). In August, the Turkish state accused Syria of supporting the PKK and refused to conduct any water negotiations (Daoudy, 2009). In any case, Erbakan was compelled to resign only twelve months after being sworn in as Prime Minister when he received a letter from the military command asking him to step down.

During the rest of the decade, Turkey changed its fluid modernity strategy with its lower riparian neighbours, as it stopped negotiating water issues with them, and shifted to only demanding their unconditional collaboration in its fight against what it considered terrorism. However, the new civilian government, resulting from an alliance between the Motherland Party (ANAP) and the Democratic Left Party (DSP), headed again by Yılmaz, made an effort to achieve a breakthrough in its relations with Syria and Iran. Turkish Foreign Minister Ismail Cem had what he called a very productive meeting with his Syrian counterpart, Faruq al-Sharaa, in March 1998. Visibly disturbed, the Turkish military criticised the government and the Foreign Minister. In a turnabout, Yılmaz visited Israel in July, where Netanyahu announced a "Turkish-Israeli axis", and the Turkish Prime Minister accused Syria of hostility toward his country (Altunisik, 2000).

The new trend culminated in October, when Turkey threatened to march into Syria with its huge NATO-trained military machine unless Damascus suppressed the PKK. Early in the month, Turkey presented Syria an ultimatum to turn Öcalan and the members of the PKK in its territory over to them. The Syrians considered the new Turkish stance surprising due to its timing, given that the PKK had just declared a unilateral ceasefire, and failed to represent a serious threat. Damascus attributed the ultimatum to Turkish domestic difficulties with the rise of the Islamist Fazilet Party, heir to then-forbidden Refah, and to Israeli instigation, which would have considered that it was the best time to get concessions from Damascus (al-Jahmani and Ousy, 1999). Indeed, that year al-Asad, already severely ill, had made important purges in the summit of the Syrian leadership to smooth the process of having his son Bashar succeed him (Sezgin, 2002). Hafiz al-Asad decided to submit and had Öcalan put on a plane out of the country. With the help of US and Israeli intelligence services, Turkish authorities managed to arrest the rebel leader in 1999 and put him in an ultra-high-security prison on the island of Imralı in the Marmara Sea, where he remains at the time of writing in 2022.

4.3.2 A new governmental reason in the making

A new and more radical change took place over the first few years of the 21st century, once Bashar al-Asad took over as President of Syria. The two countries experienced an unprecedented improvement in their relations in all spheres, and signed trade, military, and cultural accords. An international governmental reason was in the making through selective negotiations and increasing trade and cooperation, while avoiding overstating the importance attributed to the interests and requests of the United States or other world or regional powers in relation to Syria. Although Turkish elites had the upper hand in numerous matters, including trade and industrial cooperation, Syrian entrepreneurs expected to see their profits grow, even if at a slower pace than those of their Turkish associates.

The regional governmental reason in the making included a water apparatus. Not only did Turkey dilute the coercive aspects of its policy, various water cooperation agreements were signed. Only thus can we make sense of the cordial evolution of water relations among the two. It should be mentioned that during his last few years in power, Saddam Hussein also avoided expressing any grudges against Turkey on the water issue. This is not really surprising, considering that sanctions and the impending US invasion were his greatest concerns. It is true, however, that the Turkish side continued to avoid negotiating and signing a definitive water treaty. Moreover, it has continued dam construction without coordinating with its lower riparian neighbours, which has more implications.

In contrast with the open conflict over water that the previous decades had witnessed, Turkish and Syrian administrations passed a Joint Communique, signed on 23 August 2001 and ratified through an Implementation Document on 19 June 2002. Although some water actions were to be coordinated, the question of the precise sharing ratio remained unresolved (Daoudy, 2009, 371). Turkey was to allow through a greater volume of fluid than that agreed in 1987, but, in times of drought, Syria would accept a lesser flow. When Ankara announced the reduction of Euphrates flow at the border because of drought in 2001, the Syrian administration expressed its understanding. It cannot be ruled out that the agreement included a tacit exchange, as the Syrian leadership stopped pushing for a tripartite water agreement including Iraq. In any case, Turkey and Syria did establish a bilateral governmental reason in which the latter got an improved trade, diplomatic and strategic relationship, while the former received land access to many markets in the Middle East, which allowed it to fabulously boost its trade in the region.

Further progress was made on the governmental reason and the water apparatus when the Islamist but neoliberal Justice and Progress Party (AKP), under the leadership of Recep Tayyip Erdoğan, came to govern Turkey. In 2004, with the signing of a bilateral Turkish-Syrian free trade agreement, Syrian Prime Minister Naji Mohammad al-Otri declared that Erdoğan, his Turkish counterpart, was committed to increasing the water flow at the border (Singh, 2005). Erdoğan confirmed the intent during his visit to Damascus in December (Araş, 2008). The new administration developed an excellent relationship with that of al-Asad, which strove to put Syria on a firm path of economic growth with increasingly neoliberal policies.

Eventually, Turkey and Syria incorporated Iraq in the water apparatus, as they went on improving their water relations, not only with the application of the new understandings, but also by promoting the establishment of a tripartite epistemic community to work on Tigris and Euphrates issues and reconvening the Joint Technical Committee. A group of scholars and water professionals from the three countries began gathering in 2005, independently of their governments, and the Joint Committee met several times starting in 2007 (Kibaroğlu and Scheumann, 2011).

It might seem paradoxical, but US-occupied Iraq was the least powerful of the states in the basin. Although excluded from the negotiations leading to the Joint Communique and the Implementation Document, Turkey and Syria brought Iraq in to common water negotiations later on. Due to the sharing agreements previously established with Syria, Iraq benefited from the flow increase and suffered from its reduction in times of drought. However, after the United States took over, neither the occupying power nor the Iraqi officials were able to negotiate on an equal footing with their neighbours or really confront them over the Tigris and Euphrates resources. One might have thought that they would use the water argument to at least put pressure on Turkey or Syria to get concessions on other issues, just as Hussein had done in the mid-1970s or Turkey and Syria during the 1980s and 1990s. However, this was not the case.

The Turkish state relaunched the GAP dam-building effort during the first decade of the 2000s, mainly on the Tigris, to re-envigorate its water apparatus in part to control its Kurdish population and in part in search for profits. After having silenced their weapons in 1999, heeding a call from Öcalan, already in prison, the PKK guerrillas went back on the offensive in 2004. Ankara responded not only by redoubling its military operations, which had continued during the militant hiatus, but also with a renewed GAP dam-building push, as the project had been hitherto considered relatively stagnant. In 2008, the Turkish and international press reported statements by officials who openly argued that the damming activity responded to the need of making jobs available and promoting prosperity in Southeast Anatolia to prevent the Kurdish population from continuing to radicalise and support the rebels (see Schleifer, 2008; Özhan, 2008). Something often skirted that should be mentioned here, is that through the first decade of the century, the PKK abandoned its former secessionist programme aiming at establishing a Socialist Kurdish state. Now, they struggle for autonomy and what they call Democratic Confederalism (Conde, 2018). Several Kurdish organisations have converged with this view, including the Kurdish Party of the Democratic Unity (PYD) in Syria.

The opposition pro-Kurdish municipal administrations in Southeast Turkey, however, asserted that State Hydraulic Works (DSI) was hiring labourers from other parts of Turkey to work on the dams and that these jobs did not benefit virtually any Kurds. Many considered the expansion of the works to be aimed at hindering the mobility of the insurgents and suppressing the population that supported them. Rather than buying off Kurds, they felt that the central government was seeking to produce a demographic change by bringing in ethnic Turks to inhabit the area.[2] If indeed the continuation of GAP aspired to incorporate Kurdish populations into the Turkish governmental reason, the scheme seems to have been a failure.

The fact is that the basin was experiencing ever more frequent droughts, and regardless of the improved downstream relations under the AKP government, Turkey continued building dams at an accelerated pace. Water stress, resulting from a combination of drought and impounding upstream dams in Turkey, has become more and more dire, to the point that Thomas Freedman had no hesitation in asserting that it became a significant factor in the outbreak and spread of the 2011 Syrian people's uprising (Friedman, 2013). Of course, Syrians had many other reasons to rebel (Conde, 2017), but that anyone could seriously believe that water stress played a key role is indicative of the gravity of the situation. Continuously building reservoirs means permanently having to impound them and therefore having less water to share with downstream riparian countries.

Iran, an upstream riparian country on a couple of Tigris tributaries, the Little Zab and the Diyala, had not been a party to Tigris and Euphrates hydropolitics during the 20th century. This, however, has changed in this century. Beginning in the early 2000s, Iran has been developing its water apparatus in the west of the country, with an impact on the water flow into Iraq. Tehran seems to hold various essentially domestic governmental reason goals, to generate profits for construction firms, make jobs available, produce hydropower for towns and industry and allow for irrigated agriculture. However, these dams seem to be affecting Kurds and Arabs, among other ethnic groups, inside Iran in ways that amount to thanatopolitics.

Internationally, however, it still seems unclear whether Iran seeks to put pressure on Iraq or it simply affects Iraq as an unintended result of its domestic water apparatus agenda. Even though Iran has sought to incorporate Iraq into its international governmental reason through other mechanisms, it seems not to be including the water apparatus as part of it. The Islamic Republic has increased its dam-building and river-diversion activities in the Tigris tributaries in the Zagros mountains, on the Little Zab and the Diyala, creating problems for downstream Iraq, including its Kurdish Region. According to local sources, Iran in the early 2020s is the third leading country in reservoir construction worldwide, with 20 dams per year in the last three decades, with substantial Asian investments (Financial Tribune, 2017). Iran has been over exploiting its groundwater resources for decades (Ashraf *et al.*, 2021), which has triggered large protests in areas such as Khuzestan and neighbouring Iraq (von Hein, 2021). The dams built or under construction along Tigris tributaries are drastically slashing the water flow into Iraq, thereby exacerbating environmental and social problems in this country (Abdulrahman, 2017), as well as in the regions in which they are built inside Iran.

4.3.3　The governmental reason breakdown

After the Arab Spring revolution broke out in Syria in March 2011, relations between the riparian countries took a new turn, and the fledgling governmental reason unravelled. Turkey and its allies supported most Syrian rebel groups opposing the al-Asad government. In Iraq, Ankara had already sided with the main opposition coalition since 2009 and entered in bilateral agreements with the Kurdistan Regional Government (KRG) in northern Iraq without going through the federal authorities in Baghdad. The KRG, meanwhile, was becoming a quasi-state actor (Castillo, 2017) that will most likely eventually develop its own water policy, although, at this writing, it still depends on Baghdad for its transnational water policy.[3] As for the Iraqi central government, it attempted a balancing act between its different and improbable allies, including the United States, Iran and Syria. However, two new hydropolitical trends appeared during the Syrian war.

A militaristic Islamic fundamentalist organisation, ISIS, tried to use the water apparatus for its own purposes, seemingly in coercive mode. While controlling extensive territories in Syria and Iraq along the Euphrates basin between at least 2014 and 2016, ISIS strove to take hold of dams with military, economic and political aims, according to reports. Some journalists (Massih, 2014; Yalqiyian, 2015) feared that control over dams could have allowed the organisation to shut off hydropower generation, significantly disrupting all kinds of activities, or deliver water to the population to gain leadership. Stergiou (2016) asserts that, by January 2015, ISIS had taken over three dams in Syria, including al-Tabqa, and sold hydropower to the Syrian government.

In Iraq, in April 2014, militants occupied the Ramadi Dam on the Euphrates and, according to Massih (2014), released a block of water that flooded land up to 100 miles downstream. The following year, Gander (2015) reported that the organisation used the reservoirs to divert the watercourse and attack government forces.

Another more stimulating novelty is the establishment in 2012–2013 of what eventually became the Autonomous Administration of North and East Syria (often referred to as Rojava) by the Kurdish movement in association with other peoples from the area. The Autonomous Administration managed to extend its influence over most of the Jazira region, which lies between the Tigris and Euphrates rivers. An anti-capitalist economy, based on social and cooperative production units, alongside private businesses, has developed (Aslan, 2021). Their agricultural and industrial activities, let alone regular household needs, require water resources, most notoriously for irrigation and hydropower generation. They have resorted to the already existing resources of the Tigris and Euphrates basin, which include its tributaries, the Balikh and the Khabur Rivers.

Turkey has employed the water apparatus with coercive objectives in the Syrian war, which also affects the lowermost riparian, Iraq. The question is at whom do they aim it. Several reports indicate a radical slash in Euphrates flows at the border town of Jarablus downstream towards Syria. Already in 2014, Anjarini (2014) denounced a flow reduction and suggested that Ankara wanted to put pressure on the internal politics of Syria. Turkish authorities denied having reduced the water flow and asserted that, on average, they had been letting 599 m^3/s through despite reports that 2014 was one of the driest years since 1961 (Turkish Republic, 2014). In June 2015, however, the Syrian minister of water told his Iraqi counterpart that during the first half of the year, the flow from Turkey had averaged 330 m^3/s, instead of the agreed 500, and that his government would continue abiding by the bilateral agreements with Iraq, thus letting 166 m^3/s through (Nassr, 2015). Karnieli *et al.* (2019) found water levels at al-Thawra dam to be severely depleted, indicating that Turkey has failed to comply with its commitments. By mid-2020 again, international reports indicated a reduction in the average flow at Jarablus down to 200 m^3/s, less than half the agreed flow (OCHA, 2020).

It appears that the Turkish State has been wielding its ability to control the water apparatus in the basin to coerce the Autonomous Administration and undermine its popularity. The Kurdish movement in Syria, particularly its largest and most influential organisations, the PYD, the People's Defence Units (YPG) and the Women's Defence Units (YPJ), is known to have ideological and political connections to the Kurdish movement in Turkey and to the PKK. It should be mentioned that the Turkish government had established a peace process with the PKK in 2013. However, in the June 2015 elections, the AKP, the party Erdoğan, lost its parliamentary majority. Shortly afterwards, clashes took place between the army and the guerrillas, and the negotiations and the truce between the two sides collapsed in July. After dissolving the parliament and an outbreak of violence in the country, new elections held in December gave the majority to AKP. In Syria, Turkey turned from supporting large sections of the Syrian rebels fighting the Bashar al-Asad government, to increasingly focusing on countering the Kurds and the Autonomous Administration. Although Turkish hostility towards it began at least in 2014, the Turkish army started attacking and occupying Syrian territory governed by the Autonomous Administration in 2016, settling, in the territories it occupied, Syrians that had taken refuge in Turkey, but who originally come from other parts of their country.

Turkey seems to have utilised the water apparatus against the Autonomous Administration in several ways. The reduction of Euphrates water flow has most notoriously affected the Autonomous Administration. Since up to 80% of electricity consumed in the Jazira comes from hydropower (Christou, 2020), the diminishing volumes in hydroelectric dams hinder the availability not only of the fluid but of power for all sorts of activities. In 2019, of the total population there, 2.2 million lived in areas that were part of the Administration, and 450,000 in towns partly controlled by the Syrian government. These figures included 900,000 internally displaced persons (ACAPS, 2019) from the areas occupied by Turkey and from other parts of Syria, not to mention refugees from Iraq.

This same year, Turkey largely increased its water abstractions from the sources of the Balikh and the Khabur. Karnieli *et al.* (2019) found that this has severely harmed crops. Also in 2019, in a Turkey-occupied area, an important pumping station delivering water to almost half a million people was damaged (Human Rights Watch, 2020). Despite calls on the Turkish government by humanitarian organisations to repair it, towards the end of 2021, it was still operating at suboptimal levels (Holleis, 2021; Humanitarian Response, 2021; FAO, 2021). The economy of peasants has been harshly affected, and many have been driven to abandon agriculture altogether (FAO, 2021). These actions by Turkey have taken a high toll on an already gravely deteriorated humanitarian situation in war-ravaged Syria.

An outstanding member of the PYD and of its women section, Asya Abdullah, said that Turkey, in each of its invasions of Northern Syria, in 2016, 2018 and 2019, has engaged in ethnic cleansing. "Now they use the water weapon to spoil the life of people and push them to leave" (den Hond, 2021).

4.4 Conclusions

It seems quite clear that fluid modernity and hydropolitics took an important turn in the Middle East after 1990. The difference lies not in the fact that domestic and international water mechanisms were being developed or that they were part of governmentality. All this is constitutive of fluid modernity. The difference is that, unlike the years going from 1956 to 1990 (covered in Chapter 3), during the period inaugurated in 1991, some of the stronger states, including the United States, Turkey and even Israel, believed it possible to use the water apparatus (among others) to broaden their international governmental reason and to integrate new states into it, just like the United States had hoped to achieve in the early 1950s (Chapter 2). However, this proved more elusive than expected. Even Jordan was never entirely satisfied with the limited Israeli compliance with the 1994 water agreement. To this, it should be added that many Jordanian citizens are also Palestinians, which makes them extremely sensitive to events in Israel, the West Bank and Gaza, whether related to water, land, human rights, equal rights, peace or other topics. Turkey did eventually achieve a breakthrough with Syria, but it only continued while stability lasted in this country. Iran, a relative newcomer to Middle Eastern international water apparatuses, is a case of its own, apparently not yet seeking to integrate this dispositif into the governmentality that it has developed with Iraq.

As for the within-borders water apparatus in states with large oppressed national minorities, at least Israel and Turkey, the practice seems to have differed from one case to another. Under the sway of internationally promoted negotiations, Israel sought to integrate with the Palestinian Authority in managing a water apparatus to administer the life of West Bank and Gaza Palestinians. However, the reality of this water apparatus is that of a special one, different than the apparatus for Israelis, which means that the Palestinians live under the rule of the state of emergency for the oppressed, which is of course unbearable. Water stands high in their list of grievances. A relatively similar situation afflicts Kurds. Turkey has developed the water apparatus in the regions most densely inhabited by Kurds in the country in a way that seems less an administration of life than a way of policing them and excluding them from the governmental-reason paradigm.

An interesting novelty after the peoples' rebellions of 2011 in the region is the practice of hydropolitics by opposition organisations. One is ISIS and the use it made of water and dams under their control, which was more similar to the establishment of both a bio and a thanatopolitics. A more interesting case, in a totally different sense, is perhaps the Autonomous Administration of North and East Syria, that requires water to prop an alternative economy based on cooperatives and self-rule. However, it finds itself under attack by, among other foes, Turkey not only through the security dispositif, but also through the water apparatus, and to extremes seldom seen elsewhere.

Notes

1 See the UN Office for the Coordination of Humanitarian Affairs in the Occupied Palestinian Territories map at www.ochaopt.org/atlas2019/wbclos ure.html and reports such as OCHA-oPT (2014) and OCHA-oPT (2007).
2 Author interview with Abdullah Demirbaş, Mayor of Sur, a district of Diyarbakir, May 29, 2013 (Conde, 2016). The mere statement of the question made Mr. Demirbaş grin in disbelief.
3 Conclusions of the author after interviewing Mohammed Amin Faris, Director General of Water Resources, Ministry of Irrigation and Water Resources, KRG, 12 June 2013.

Epilogue

This book proposes a radical, critical take on hydropolitics. It examines social water relations with an eye on history, social space, power and culture, sometimes even among states, while keeping in mind, explicitly or otherwise, relations of property, class, race, gender, religion, empire and nation, and always with the oppressed, the subaltern subjects, at the centre of its reflections.

What by definition goes for water, its being fluid "under normal conditions of pressure and temperature", quite largely goes for fluid modernity. Water produced through technology—nature gone artificial in the Anthropocene, water automatically at hand—has become the normal everyday reality that virtually nobody really thinks about. The ultimate questions at stake, however, relate not to whether fluid modernity is good or bad, but how and for what purposes it is used. Is the goal to satisfy the needs of everyone without completely spoiling the conditions for others (and other species)? Or is it simply about the few making profits and administering life for the many, but less so for many others, and without really thinking about life in the holistic, qualitative sense of the term?

Humans, capital, states, nations have sought to control fluidity through interventions in space, by developing colossal pieces of infrastructure, grandiose plans and schemes, discourses, imaginations, comfort, with the aim of achieving progress, modernity, development, the nation, peace in doses, earnings and power. Water technologies and discourses, and the fluid itself, have been turned into a central part of a power mechanism, the water apparatus, that has served many purposes beyond being simply a first iteration of profit making. The water apparatus contributed to the governmental reason locally, regionally, and globally to turn power into a more or less subtle device of self-producing and reproducing discipline. Hydro-hegemony, water domination *versus* consensus, hard power *versus* soft power all get integrated into the water apparatus and the overall governmental reason.

However, when governmentality fails to produce self-discipline among sections of society, nation-states resort to states of emergency, spaces of exception, and the openly coercive instruments of the security apparatus to impose discipline on them. The water apparatus also includes security enforcing aspects that overlap the former. Populations may be deprived of the fluid or other benefits of the water dispositif.

The mechanism seems to turn more smoothly within borders than across them. The task was made easier by the discourse of progress, development and modernity, so tied to the rise and reproduction of nationalism in postcoloniality. Domestic opposition, if viable, would have to deal with the governmental reason, with administering life without even having to think about it or making a choice. In some cases, here exemplified by Israel and Turkey, the water apparatus not only could generate self-reproducing discipline among fully recognised nationals but also impose discipline on those considered outsiders, excluded from the nation, Palestinians and Kurds, sent to the spaces of exception, where life is administered, but in dribs and drabs.

In the international arena, the water apparatus and the governmental reason have operated with mixed results to bring forth a self-reproducing discipline by states or to impose discipline upon them. In the beginning of the Cold War, the terms of postcoloniality were being worked out. The Eisenhower Administration sought to get Arab states to join the Western Alliance and accept peace with Israel on its terms through the Johnston water negotiation process. Funding for monumental water development projects was offered to most states in the region. When Nasser and al-Quwatli concluded that they could only build their defence system through Eastern Bloc aid, the entire US water-apparatus proposals to Egypt and Syria were taken off the table. The rebellious new states found in the alternative world super power, the Soviet Union, the necessary funding and expertise to continue their course towards full-fledged fluid modernity. A period of renegotiation of the terms of independence and sovereignty, of postcoloniality, followed, in which coercion was the key of a state of emergency governmental reason for states that failed to accommodate.

Fluid modernity, it needs to be stressed, is not only a process in which corporations make profits, or states get populations or other states to self-discipline through the water apparatus. The subalterns are active subjects. In some cases, like the ones discussed in this book, quite sizeable groups manage to organise and rebel, and produce their own fluid frames and practices. This is seen in Palestinian and Kurdish liberation movements and beyond.

Some seek to achieve emancipation and materialise some degrees of utopia, like the Autonomous Administration of North and East Syria. They try to use water and water technology to satisfy social needs while breaking out of the governmental reasons of the state in which they live and those surrounding them. All but easy, the task has paid off, at least in terms of challenging the dominant governmentality of certain states. Several forces, including the Turkish and Syrian states and ISIS, try to break them. Ankara has flexed the water apparatus in coercive mode against them, severely worsening, in the process, an already terrible humanitarian crisis.

In this book, I have discussed the fluid-modernity biopolitics of water, aided by a handful of empirical cases from a very delimited area of the world that hopeful will suffice to show the usefulness of the approach. The world of fluid modernity, however, is much broader than this. Many social practices related to water could be studied from this perspective. A few come to my mind: The Peace and Democracy Party (BDP) practice in Diyarbakir, Batman and other municipalities in Southeast Anatolia, to distribute the fluid without charging a fee since they consider access to water a human right; the Bolivian social struggles (dubbed "Cochabamba Water Wars") in 2000 against the privatisation of water to transnational utilities corporations; the fight against the building of La Parota Dam in the Mexican state of Guerrero. Many more could be added, in terms of activities, themes, scales, time frames. The politics of fluid modernity point to yet another link binding the fate of humankind together, despite the particularities of regional politics.

Bibliography

Abdulrahman, Salam Abdulqadir, Nov. 2017, "The Drying up of the Lower Zab River and Future Water Disputes between Iran, Kurdistan Region and Iraq", *International Journal of Environmental Studies*, vol. 75, no. 1, 29–44 (www.tandfonline.com/doi/pdf/10.1080/00207233.2017.1406725).

Aboites, Luis, 1998, *El agua de la nación: una historia política de México (1888–1946)*. Mexico, Centro de Investigaciones y Estudios Superiores en Antropología Social.

ACAPS, 21 Oct. 2019, "Syria: displacement in the northeast", Briefing note (www.acaps.org/sites/acaps/files/products/files/20191021_acaps_start_briefing_note_syria_displacement_in_the_northeast.pdf).

Achcar, Gilbert, 2013, *Marxism, orientalism, cosmopolitanism*. London, Saqi.

Achcar, Gilbert and Michel Warschawski, 2006, *La guerre des 33 jours: la guerre d'Israël contre le Hezbollah au Liban et ses conséquences*. Paris, Textuel. Collection La discorde.

Agamben, Giorgio, 1998, *Homo Sacer: sovereign power and bare life*. Redwood City, Stanford University Press, trans. from Italian by Daniel Heller-Roazen.

Agamben, Giorgio, 2005, *State of exception*. Chicago, University Of Chicago Press, trans. from Italian by Kevin Attel.

Akgul, Bartug Kemal, Jun. 2014, *Social Network Analysis of Construction Companies Operating in International Markets: The Case of Turkish Contractors*, M.A. Thesis, Ankara, The Graduate School of Natural and Applied Sciences, Middle East Technical University (https://open.metu.edu.tr/bitstream/handle/11511/23600/index.pdf).

Akhter, Majed, May 2015, "The Hydropolitical Cold War: The Indus Waters Treaty and State Formation in Pakistan", *Political Geography*, vol. 46, 65–75 (www.sciencedirect.com/science/article/pii/S0962629814001255).

al-Jahmani, Yusuf Ibrahim and Salar Ousy, 1999, *Turkiya wa-Suriya*. Damascus, Dar Houran. No. 2 in Malaffaat Turkiya.

Al-Taani, Ahmed A., 2013, "Seasonal Variations in Water Quality of Al-Wehda Dam North of Jordan and Water Suitability for Irrigation in Summer", *Arabian Journal of Geosciences*, vol. 6, no. 4, 1131–1140 (https://doi.org/10.1007/s12517-011-0428-y).

Alatout, Samer, Jan. 2008, "'States' of Scarcity: Water, Space, and Identity Politics in Israel, 1948–59", *Environment and Planning D: Society and Space*, vol. 26, no. 6, 959–982.

Allan, J. Anthony, 2001, *The Middle East water question: hydropolitics and the global economy*. London, I.B. Tauris, International Library of Human Geography.

Allouche, Jeremy, Jun. 2020, "Nationalism, Legitimacy and Hegemony in Transboundary Water Interactions", *Water Alternatives*, vol. 13, no. 2, 286–301 (www.water-alternatives.org/index.php/alldoc/articles/volume-13/issue-2/576-a13-2-5/file).

Alon, Gideon, 20 Jan. 2004, "PM: Talking to Syria will lose us Golan", Haaretz. com (www.haaretz.com/print-edition/news/pm-talking-to-syria-will-lose-us-golan-1.111525).

Alpher, Yossi, 2015, *Periphery: Israel's search for Middle East Allies*. Lanham, Rowman & Littlefield Publishers.

Altunisik, Meliha, Apr. 2000, "The Turkish-Israeli Rapprochement in the Post-Cold War Era", *Middle Eastern Studies*, vol. 36, no. 2, 172–191 (www.tandfonline.com/doi/abs/10.1080/00263200008701313).

Amery, Hussein, 2000, "A Popular Theory of Water Diversion from Lebanon: Toward Public Participation for Peace", in Hussein Amery and Aaron T. Wolf, eds., *A geography of peace: water in the Middle East*, Austin, Texas University Press, 121–149.

Amnesty International, 2022, *Israel's Apartheid against Palestinians: Cruel System of Domination and Crime against Humanity*, Amnesty International (www.amnesty.org/en/wp-content/uploads/2022/02/MDE1551412022 ENGLISH.pdf).

Anand, Nikhil, Akhil Gupta and Hannah Appel, 2018, *The promise of infrastructure*. Durham, Duke University Press. A School for Advanced Research Advanced Seminar.

Anjarini, Suhaib, 30 May 2014, "A new Turkish aggression against Syria: Ankara suspends pumping Euphrates' water", Al Akhbar English (http://english.al-akhbar.com/node/19970).

Appel, Hannah, Nikhil Anand and Akhil Gupta, 2018, "Introduction: Temporality, Politics, and the Promise of Infrastructure", in Nikhil Anand, Akhil Gupta and Hannah Appel, eds., *The promise of infrastructure*. Durham, Duke University Press, 1–38. A School for Advanced Research Advanced Seminar.

Araş, Bülent, May 2008, "Turkey between Syria and Israel: Turkey's Rising Soft Power", *Policy Brief*, no. 15 (ciaotest.cc.columbia.edu/pbei/seta/0001299/0001299.pdf).

Ashraf, Samaneh, Ali Nazemi and Amir AghaKouchak, Apr. 2021, "Anthropogenic Drought Dominates Groundwater Depletion in Iran", *Scientific Reports*, vol. 11, no. 1, 9135 (https://doi.org/10.1038/s41598-021-88522-y).

Aslan, Azize, 2021, *Economía anticapitalista en Rojava: las contradicciones de la revolución en la lucha kurda*. Guadalajara, Cátedra Jorge Alonso.

Ayeb, Habib, 1998, *L'eau au Proche-Orient: la guerre n'aura pas lieu*. Paris, Karthala.

Barnet, Richard J., 1980, *The lean years: politics in the age of scarcity*. New York, Simon and Schuster.

Beaumont, Peter, 2000, "Conflict, Coexistence, and Cooperation: A Study of Water Use in the Jordan Basin", in Hussein Amery and Aaron T. Wolf, eds., *A geography of peace: water in the Middle East*, Austin, Texas University Press, 19–44.

Beaumont, Peter, 29 Apr. 2014, "Israel risks becoming Apartheid state if peace talks fail, says John Kerry", The Guardian.

Benjamin, Walter, 1989, "Theses on the Philosophy of History", in Stephen Eric Bronner and Douglas Kellner, eds., *Critical theory and society: a reader*, New York, Routledge, 255–263.

Benziman, Uri, 16 Sep. 2002, "Some want water, some want fire", Haaretz (www.haaretz.com/print-edition/opinion/some-want-fire-some-want-water-1.34180).

Biswas, Asit K., John F. Kolars, Masahiro Murakami, John Waterbury and Aaron T. Wolf, 1997, *Core and periphery: a comprehensive approach to Middle Eastern water*. Delhi, Oxford University Press. Water Resources Management Series, 5.

Boyer, Dominic, 2018, "Infrastructure, Potential Energy, Revolution", in Nikhil Anand, Akhil Gupta and Hannah Appel, eds., *The promise of infrastructure*, Durham, Duke University Press, 223–243. A School for Advanced Research Advanced Seminar.

Bulloch, John and Adel Darwish, 1993, *Water wars: coming conflicts in the Middle East*. London, Victor Gollancz.

Bush, George H. W., Sep. 1990, *September 11, 1990: Address before a Joint Session of Congress*, Miller Center, University of Virginia (https://millercen ter.org/the-presidency/presidential-speeches/september-11-1990-address-joint-session-congress).

Bush, George H. W., Mar. 1991, *March 6, 1991: Address Before a Joint Session of Congress on the End of the Gulf War*, Miller Center, University of Virginia (https://millercenter.org/the-presidency/presidential-speeches/march-6-1991-address-joint-session-congress-end-gulf-war).

Campbell, Ian C., Nov. 2016, "Integrated Management in the Mekong River Basin", *Ecohydrology & Hydrobiology*, vol. 16, no. 4, 255–262 (www.scienc edirect.com/science/article/pii/S1642359316300428).

Castillo, Juan Carlos, otoño 2017, "¿Estatalidad de facto o autonomismo democrático? El proyecto político de los kurdos en Siria e Irak", *Istor*, vol. 18, no. 70, 51–72.

Chalabi, Hasan and Tarek Majzoub, 1995, "Turkey, the Waters of the Euphrates and Public International Law", in John Anthony Allan and Chibli Mallat, eds., *Water in the Middle East: legal, political and commercial implications*, London, I.B. Tauris, 189–232.

Chesnot, Christian, 1993, *La bataille de l'eau au Proche-Orient*. Paris, L'Harmattan.

Christou, Will, Aug. 2020, *Turkish dams threaten northeast Syria with ecological and economic blight*. Syria Direct (https://syriadirect.org/turkish-dams-threa ten-northeast-syria-with-ecological-and-economic-blight/).

Cobban, Helena, 1999, *The Israeli-Syrian peace talks: 1991-96 and beyond*. Washington, United States Institute of Peace Press.

Conde, Gilberto, 2013, "Turquía e Iraq en las cambiantes relaciones internacionales de Siria", in Luis Mesa Delmonte, ed., *Las Relaciones Exteriores de Siria*. Mexico, El Colegio de México, 159–205.

Conde, Gilberto, Jan. 2016, "Water and Counter-Hegemony: Kurdish Views on Tigris and Euphrates Water Management in Turkey", *Revista de Paz y Conflictos*, vol. 9, no. 2, 43–58 (http://revistaseug.ugr.es/index.php/revpaz/ article/view/5319).

Conde, Gilberto, Jun. 2017, "On the Evolutions of the Arab Spring", *Regions and Cohesion*, vol. 7, no. 2, 96–105 (www.berghahnjournals.com/journals/ regions-and-cohesion/7/2/reco070206.xml).

Conde, Gilberto, 2018, "Comparer les rébélions kurde et zapatiste", in Bernard Botiveau, Hernando Salcedo Fidalgo and Aude Signoles, eds., *Amérique latine – Monde arabe. La diagonale des Suds*, Paris, Riveneuve, 119–140 (www.riveneuve.com/en/catalogue/amerique-latine-monde-arabe-la-diagon ale-des-suds/).

CSWSME, Committee on Sustainable Water Supplies in the Middle East, 1999, *Water for the future: the West Bank and Gaza Strip, Israel, and Jordan*. Washington, National Academies Press.

Cullather, Nick, Sep. 2002, "Damming Afghanistan: Modernization in a Buffer State", *The Journal of American History*, vol. 89, no. 2, 512 (https://acade mic.oup.com/jah/article-abstract/89/2/512/755839).

Daoudy, Marwa, 2005, *Le partage des eaux entre la Syrie, l'Irak et la Turquie: Négociation, sécurité et asymétrie des pouvoirs*. Paris, CNRS. Moyen-Orient.

Daoudy, Marwa, 2008, "Hydro-Hegemony and International Water Law: Laying Claims to Water Rights", *Water Policy*, vol. 10, no. Supplement 2, 89–102.

Daoudy, Marwa, 2009, "Asymmetric Power: Negotiating Water in the Euphrates and Tigris", *International Negotiation*, vol. 14, no. 2, 361–391 (http://gradua teinstitute.ch/webdav/site/political_science/shared/political_science/4958/ InternationalNegotiation-Daoudy.pdf).

den Hond, Chris, Oct. 2021, "La Turquie mène une guerre de l'eau en Syrie", Orient XXI (https://orientxxi.info/magazine/la-turquie-mene-une-guerre- de-l-eau-en-syrie,5084).

Derfner, Larry, 30 Jul. 2001, "The Littlest Casualty", *U.S. News & World Report*, vol. 131, no. 4 (www.usnews.com/usnews/news/articles/010730/arc hive_038046.htm).

Dinmore, Eric, 2013, "Concrete Results? The TVA and the Appeal of Large Dams in Occupation-Era Japan", *The Journal of Japanese Studies*, vol. 39, no. 1, 1–38 (www.jstor.org/stable/24242584).

Dodge, Toby and Tariq Tell, 1996, "Peace and the Politics of Water in Jordan", in John Anthony Allan ed., *Water, peace and the Middle East: negotiating resources in the Jordan Basin*, London, I.B. Tauris, 169–184. Library of Modern Middle East Studies, 9.

Dolatyar, Mostafa and Tim S. Gray, 1999, *Water politics in the Middle East: a context for conflict or cooperation?*. New York, Palgrave Macmillan.

Domínguez, Judith, 2019, "La construcción de presas en México. Evolución, situación actual y nuevos enfoques para dar viabilidad a la infraestructura hídrica", *Gestión y política pública*, vol. 28, no. 1, 3–37 (http://hdl.handle.net/11651/2965).

Dube, Saurabh, 2017, *Subjects of modernity: time-space, disciplines, margins*. Manchester, Manchester University Press. Theory for a global age.

Dussel, Enrique, 2014, *Filosofías del Sur y Descolonización*, Buenos Aires, Editorial Docencia.

Ecosoc, UN Economic and Social Council, 4 Feb. 1997, *Comprehensive Assessment of the Freshwater Resources of the World*, Ecosoc (www.un.org/esa/documents/ecosoc/cn17/1997/ecn171997-9.htm).

Elhance, Arun P., Apr. 1997, "Conflict and Cooperation over Water in the Aral Sea Basin", *Studies in Conflict & Terrorism*, vol. 20, no. 2, 207–218.

Elmas, Hasan Basri, 1999, *Turquie-Europe: une relation ambiguë*. Paris, Syllepse. Points Cardinaux.

Engin, Nazin, 1997, "Perspectives for Improvement in Arab-Turkish Economic Cooperation", in Fatin Al-Bustani, ed., *The Arab World and Turkey: economy and regional security*, Amman, The Arab Thought Forum/Friedrich Ebert Stiftung, 12–20. Arab-international dialogues.

FAO, Dec. 2021, *Special Report: 2021 FAO Crop and Food Supply Assessment Mission to the Syrian Arab Republic*, Rome, Food and Agriculture Organisation of the United Nations (https://reliefweb.int/report/syrian-arab-republic/special-report-2021-fao-crop-and-food-supply-assessment-mission-syrian).

Financial Tribune, Mar. 2017, "S. Koreans, Chinese Companies to Develop Hydroelectric Dams in Iran", *Financial Tribune* (https://financialtribune.com/node/61409).

Fischhendler, Itay, Jan 2008, "Ambiguity in Transboundary Environmental Dispute Resolution: The Israeli–Jordanian Water Agreement", *Journal of Peace Research*, vol. 45, no. 1, 91–109 (https://doi.org/10.1177/0022343307084925).

Foucault, Michel, 1971, *L'ordre du discours*. Paris, Gallimard.

Foucault, Michel, 10 Jan. 1979, "La critique de la raison gouvernementale", France culture: Cours de Michel Foucault au Collège de France 1/5 (www.franceculture.fr/philosophie/cours-de-michel-foucault-au-college-de-france-15-la-critique-de-la-raison).

Foucault, Michel, 2008, *The birth of biopolitics: lectures at the College de France, 1978-79*. Basingstoke, Palgrave Macmillan, trans. from French by Graham Burchell.

Foundation for Middle East Peace, Nov.-Dec. 2001, "West Bank and Gaza Strip Settlement Facts-January-June 2001", *Special Report*, vol. 11, no. 6 (www.fmep.org/reports/2001/v11n6.html).

Friedman, SGM Herbert A. (Ret.), 14 Aug. 2006, *Psychological Operations during the Israel-Lebanon War 2006* (www.psywar.org/israellebanon.php).

Friedman, Thomas, 19 May 2013, "Without water revolution", The New York Times (www.nytimes.com/2013/05/19/opinion/sunday/friedman-without-water-revolution.html).

Gander, Kashmira, 3 Jun. 2015, "ISIS militants use water as weapon of war in Iraq by shutting dam on the Euphrates River", The Independent (www.independent.co.uk/news/world/middle-east/isis-use-water-as-a-weapon-in-iraq-by-shutting-dam-on-the-euphrates-river-10295763.html).

GAP-RDA, Southeast Anatolia Project, Regional Development Administration, Jun. 2006, *Latest Situation on Southeastern Anatolia Project: Activities of the gap Administration*, GAP Regional Development Administration (http://includes.gap.gov.tr/files/ek-dosyalar\s\do6(e)n/about-gap/latest-situation.pdf).

Gerges, Fawaz A., 1994, *The superpowers and the Middle East: regional and international politics, 1955-1967*. Boulder, Westview Press.

Gibbs, Leah M, Jan. 2010, "'A Beautiful Soaking Rain': Environmental Value and Water beyond Eurocentrism", *Environment and Planning D: Society and Space*, vol. 28, no. 2, 363–378 (https://journals.sagepub.com/doi/abs/10.1068/d9207).

Gleick, Peter H., Sep. 1992, *Water and conflict*. Toronto, University of Toronto. Project on Environmental Change and Acute Conflict, Occasional Paper Series, 1.

Gleick, Peter H., 2000, *The world's water: 2000-2001 (The biennial report on freshwater resources)*. Washington, Island Press.

Gramsci, Antonio, 1971, *Selections from the prison notebooks of Antonio Gramsci*. New York, International Publishers, edited and trans. from Italian by Quintin Hoare and Geoffrey Nowell-Smith.

Gramsci, Antonio, 2000, *The Gramsci reader: selected writings, 1916-1935*. New York, New York University Press, edited by David Forgasc.

Gómez, Anahí, Lucrecia Wagner, Beatriz Torres, Facundo Martín and Facundo Rojas, 2014, "Resistencias sociales en contra de los megaproyectos hídricos en América latina", *Revista Europea de Estudios Latinoamericanos y del Caribe*, vol. 97, 75–96.

Güner, Serdar, Sep. 1998, "Signalling in the Turkish-Syrian Water Conflict", *Conflict Management and Peace Science*, vol. 16, no. 2, 185–206.

Haddadin, Munther, 1996, "Water Management: A Jordanian Viewpoint", in John Anthony Allan, ed., *Water, peace and the Middle East: negotiating resources in the Jordan Basin*, New York, St. Martin's Press, 59–73.

Haddadin, Munther J., Mar. 2011, "Water: Triggering Cooperation between Former Enemies", *Water International*, vol. 36, no. 2, 178–185.

Hamilton, Richard E, 1969, "Damodar Valley Corporation: India's Experiment with the TVA Model", *Indian Journal of Public Administration*, vol. 15, no. 1, 86–109.

Harvey, David, 2001, *Spaces of capital: towards a critical geography*. New York, Routledge.

Harvey, Penelope, Casper Bruun Jensen and Atsuro Morita, 2017, "Introduction: Infrastructural Complications", in Penelope Harvey, Casper Bruun Jensen and Atsuro Morita, eds., *Infrastructures and social complexity: a companion*, London and New York, Routledge, 1–22.

Hawkins, Gay, Jan. 2011, "Making Water into a Political Material: The Case of PET Bottles", *Environment and Planning A: Economy and Space*, vol. 43, no. 9, 2001–2006 (https://journals.sagepub.com/doi/pdf/10.1068/a44306).

Herrera Santana, David, Apr. 2019, "Geopolítica de la fragmentación y poder infraestructural. El Proyecto 'One Belt, One Road' y América Latina", *Geopolítica(s)*. *Revista de estudios sobre espacio y poder*, vol. 10, no. 1, 41–68 (https://doi.org/10.5209/geop.58761).

Herrera Santana, David, 2020, "La geopolítica y la crítica. Lo político y lo geopolítico", in David Herrera, ed., *Geopolítica. Espacio, poder y resistencias en el siglo XXI*, Madrid and Mexico, Trama Editorial, UNAM, 9–42.

Hillel, Daniel, 1994, *Rivers of Eden: the struggle for water and the quest for peace in the Middle East*. New York, Oxford University Press.

Hoag, Heather J., Dec. 2006, "Transplanting the TVA? International Contributions to Postwar River Development in Tanzania", *Comparative Technology Transfer and Society*, vol. 4, no. 3, 247–267 (https://doi.org/10.1353/ctt.2007.0005).

Hobsbawm, Eric J., 2008, *On empire: America, war, and global supremacy*. New York, Pantheon Books.

Hof, Frederic C., 2022, *Reaching for the heights: the inside story of a secret attempt to reach a Syrian-Israeli peace*. Washington, United States Institute of Peace Press.

Hof, Frederic C., 2000, "The Water Dimension of Golan Heights Negotiations", in Hussein Amery and Aaron T. Wolf, eds., *A geography of peace: water in the Middle East*, London, Texas University Press, 150–167.

Holleis, Jennifer, Jan. 2021, "Syria: Are water supplies being weaponized by Turkey?" (www.dw.com/en/syria-are-water-supplies-being-weaponized-by-turkey/a-56314995).

Horkheimer, Max and Theodor W. Adorno, 2002, *Dialectic of enlightenment: philosophical fragments*. Stanford, Stanford University Press, edited by Gunzelin Schmid Noerr, trans. from German by Edmund Jephcott.

Horner, John E., 1948, "Future of Palestine [Memorandum]", in United States Department of State, ed., *Foreign relations of the United States, 1948. The Near East, South Asia, and Africa (in two parts)*, Washington, U.S. Government Printing Office, vol. V, 898 and ff., (http://digital.library.wisc.edu/1711.dl/FRUS.FRUS1948v05p2), part 2, doc. 213.

Human Rights Watch, Mar. 2020, "Turkey/Syria: weaponizing water in global pandemic?", Human Rights Watch (www.hrw.org/news/2020/03/31/turkey/syria-weaponizing-water-global-pandemic).

Human Rights Watch, Apr. 2021, "A threshold crossed Israeli authorities and the crimes of Apartheid and persecution", Human Rights Watch (www.hrw.org/sites/default/files/media_2021/04/israel_palestine0421_web_0.pdf).

Humanitarian Response, Sep. 2021, *Water crisis in Northern and Northeast Syria: Immediate Response and Funding Requirements*, Humanitarian Response (www.humanitarianresponse.info/en/operations/whole-of-syria/document/water-crisis-northern-and-northeast-syria-immediate-response-and).

IBRD, International Bank for Reconstruction and Development, 1955, *The economic development of Syria*. Baltimore, The Johns Hopkins Press (www-wds.worldbank.org/external/default/WDSContentServer/WDSP/IB/2003/01/08/000178830_98101911133036/Rendered/INDEX/multi0page.txt).

Inan, Yüksel, 1994, "Legal Dimensions of International Watercourse (Euphrates and Tigris)", in Ali Ihsan Bağış, ed., *Water as an element of cooperation and development in the Middle East*, Istanbul, Ayna/Hacettepe Universitesi/Friedrich Naumann Foundation, 223–237.

Ives, Peter and Nicola Short, 2013, "On Gramsci and the International: A Textual Analysis", *Review of International Studies*, vol. 39, no. 3, 621–642.

Jansen, Michael, 17–23 Oct. 2002, "Southern thirst", Al Ahram Weekly, Cairo, no. 608 (http://weekly.ahram.org.eg/2002/608/re6.htm).

Jongerden, Joost, Mar. 2010, "Dams and Politics in Turkey: Utilizing Water, Developing Conflict", *Middle East Policy*, vol. 17, no. 1, 137–143, (https://doi.org/10.1111/j.1475-4967.2010.00432.x).

Joyce, Patrick, 2003, *The rule of freedom: liberalism and the modern city*. London, Verso.

Kally, Elisha (with Gideon Fishelson), 1993, *Water and peace: water resources and the Arab-Israeli peace process*. Westport, Praeger.

Kankal, Murat, Sinan Nacar and Ergun Uzlu, Nov. 2016, "Status of Hydropower and Water Resources in the Southeastern Anatolia Project (GAP) of Turkey", *Energy Reports*, vol. 2, 123–128 (www.sciencedirect.com/science/article/pii/S2352484716300166).

Karnieli, Arnon, Alexandra Shtein, Natalya Panov, Noam Weisbrod and Alon Tal, Jul. 2019, "Was Drought Really the Trigger Behind the Syrian Civil War in 2011?", *Water*, vol. 11, no. 8, 1564.

Kauffer, Edith, ed., 2018, *Cuencas transfronterizas: la apertura de la presa del nacionalismo metodológico*. Mexico, Centro de Investigación y Estudios Superiores en Antropología Social (CIESAS). Biblioteca del agua.

Kay, Paul A. and Bruce Mitchell, 2000, "Water Security for the Jordan River States: Performance Criteria and Uncertainty", in Hussein Amery and Aaron T. Wolf, eds., *A geography of peace: water in the Middle East*, Austin, Texas University Press, 168–190.

Kenworthy, E.W., 3 Jul. 1965, "U.S. to Lend Turks $40 million for big Euphrates dam project; France, Italy, Germany and 2 agencies also will help meet $331 million cost", The New York Times (https://timesmachine.nytimes.com/timesmachine/1965/07/03/94965332.html?pageNumber=2).

Kerr, Malcolm Hooper, 1967, *The Arab Cold War 1958–1967: a study of ideology in politics*. 2nd ed., London, Oxford University Press.

Khalidi, Rashid, 2009, *Sowing crisis: the cold war and American Dominance in the Middle East*. Boston, Beacon Press.

KHRP, Kurdish Human Rights Project, The Ilısu Dam Campaign and The Corner House, Jul. 2002, "Downstream impacts of Turkish dam construction on Syria and Iraq: joint report of fact-finding mission to Syria and

Iraq", The Corner House, London (www.thecornerhouse.org.uk/pdf/docum ent/IraqSyri.pdf).

Kibaroğlu, Ayşegül and I.H. Olcay Ünver, 2000, "An Institutional Framework for Facilitating Cooperation in the Euphrates-Tigris River Basin", *International Negotiation: A Journal of Theory and Practice*, vol. 5, no. 2, 311–330 (www.gap.metu.edu.tr/html/yayinlar/an_institutional_framework_ AKibaroglu.pdf).

Kibaroğlu, Ayşegül, 2002, *Building a regime for the waters of the Euphrates-Tigris River Basin.* London, Kluwer Law International. International and National Water Law and Policy Series.

Kibaroğlu, Ayşegül and Waltina Scheumann, 2011, "Euphrates-Tigris Rivers System: Political Rapprochement and Transboundary Water Cooperation", in Ayşegül Kibaroğlu, Waltina Scheumann and Annika Kramer, eds., *Turkey's water policy: national frameworks and international cooperation*, Berlin, Springer, 277–299.

Klare, Michael T., 2001, *Resource wars: the new landscape of global conflict.* New York, Owl Books, 2001.

Klein, Christine A, Fall 1999, "On Dams and Democracy", *Oregon Law Review*, vol. 78, 641 (https://ssrn.com/abstract=1266162).

Kliot, Nurit, 1994, *Water resources and conflict in the Middle East.* London, Routledge.

Kliot, Nurit, 2000, "A Cooperative Framework for Sharing Scarce Water Resources: Israel, Jordan, and the Palestinian Authority", in Hussein Amery and Aaron T. Wolf, eds., *A geography of peace: water in the Middle East*, Austin, Texas University Press, 191–217.

Kolars, John F. and William A. Mitchell, 1991, *The Euphrates River and the South East Anatolia development project.* Carbondale and Edwardsville, Southern Illinois University Press. Geography.

Kolko, Gabriel, 2006, *The age of war: the United States confronts the world.* Boulder and London, Lynne Rienner.

Krishna, Raj, 1995, "International Watercourses: World Bank Experience and Policy", in John Anthony Allan and Chibli Mallat, eds., *Water in the Middle East: legal, political and commercial implications*, London, I.B. Tauris, 29–54.

Kumral, Mehmet Akif, 2016, *Rethinking Turkey-Iraq relations: the dilemma of partial cooperation.* New York, Palgrave Macmillan. Middle East today.

Lefebvre, Henri, 2000, *La production de l'espace.* Paris, Anthropos. Ethnosociologie.

Lilienthal, David Eli, 1953, *TVA: democracy on the march.* 20th ed., New York, Harper.

Lonergan, Steve, 2000, "Forces of Change and the Conflict over Water in the Jordan River Basin", in Hussein Amery and Aaron T. Wolf, eds., *A geography of peace: water in the Middle East*, Austin, Texas University Press, 45–62.

Lonergan, Steve and David B. Brooks, 1994, *Watershed: the role of fresh water in the Israeli-Palestinian conflict.* Ontario, International Development Research Centre.

Lowi, Miriam R., 1995, *Water and power: the politics of a scarce resource in the Jordan River Basin*. 2nd ed., Cambridge, Cambridge University Press. Cambridge Middle East Library 31.

Löwy, Michael, 2013, *La cage d'acier: Max Weber et le marxisme wébérien*. Paris, Stock. Un ordre d'idées.

Majzoub, Tarek, 1994, *Les fleuves du Moyen-Orient*. Paris, L'Harmattan.

Marston, John and Chhuon Hoeur, 2016, "Disputas de tierras y aguas en la planicie de inundación del lago Tonlé Sap de Camboya", *Estudios de Asia y Africa*, vol. 51, no. 1 (159), 45–76.

Massih, Nadia, 21 Jul. 2014, "ISIS militants use water as weapon of war in Iraq", al-Bawaba (www.albawaba.com/news/isis-water-iraq-591811).

McCaffrey, Stephen C, 1996, "The Harmon Doctrine One Hundred Years Later: Buried, Not Praised", *Natural Resources Journal*, vol. 36, no. 4, 965–1007.

McCaffrey, Stephen C., 2001, "The Contribution of the UN Convention on the Law of the Non-Navigational Uses of International Watercourses", *International Journal of Global Environmental Issues*, vol. 1, no. 3–4, 250–263 (http://internationalwaterlaw.org/bibliography/IJGEI/03ijgenvl2001v1n 34mccaffrey.pdf).

McCully, Patrick, 2001, *Silenced rivers: the ecology and politics of large dams*. enlarged & updated ed., London, Zed Books.

McNeill, John Robert, 2000, *Something new under the sun: an environmental history of the twentieth-century world*. New York, W.W. Norton.

Menga, Filippo, Sep. 2017, "Hydropolis: Reinterpreting the Polis in Water Politics", *Political Geography*, vol. 60, 100–109 (www.sciencedirect.com/scie nce/article/pii/S0962629816302670).

Morris, Benny, 1990, *1948 and after: Israel and the Palestinians*. Oxford, Clarendon Press.

Mukerji, Chandra, 2009, *Impossible engineering: technology and territoriality on the canal du Midi*. Princeton, Princeton University Press.

Mukerji, Chandra, 2017, *Modernity reimagined?: an analytic guide*. New York, Routledge.

Mukhayam, Samer and Khaled Hijazi, 1996, *Azmat al-miyāh fī l-mintaqa al-'arabiya: al-haqā'iq wa-l-badā'il al-murākkina*. Kuwait, Al-Majlis al-Watani li-l-Thaqāfa wa-l-Funûn wa-l-Adāb. No. 209 in Silsilat Kutub Thaqāfiya Shahriya.

Murden, Simon, May 2000, "Understanding Israel's Long Conflict in Lebanon: The Search for an Alternative Approach to Security During the Peace Process", *British Journal of Middle Eastern Studies*, vol. 27, no. 1, 25–47 (https://doi.org/10.1080/13530190050010976).

Naff, Thomas and Ruth C. Matson, 1984, *Water in the Middle East: conflict or cooperation?*. Boulder, Westview Press.

Nassr, Mazen, Jun. 2015, "Water Resources Minister: Turkey violates agreements on water share", SANA, Syrian Arab News Agency (www.sana.sy/en/?p=45392).

Neff, Donald, 1994, "Israel-Syria: Conflict at the Jordan River, 1949-1967", *Journal of Palestine Studies*, vol. 13, no. 4, 26–40.

Norton, Augustus Richard, Autumn 2000, "Hizballah and the Israeli Withdrawal from Southern Lebanon", *Journal of Palestine Studies*, vol. 30, no. 1, 22–35.

Novosseloff, Alexandra and Frank Neisse, 2007, *Des murs entre les hommes*. Paris, La Documentation française.

OCHA, UN Office for the Coordination of Humanitarian Affairs, Jul. 2020, "Syrian Arab Republic North East Syria: Al Hol camp", OCHA Services Relief Web (https://reliefweb.int/report/syrian-arab-republic/syrian-arab-republic-north-east-syria-al-hol-camp-26-july-2020).

OCHA-oPT, United Nations Office for the Coordination of Humanitarian Affairs - Occupied Palestinian Territory, Nov. 2007, "OCHA special focus: the barrier gate and permit regime four years on: humanitarian impact in the northern West Bank", OCHA Occupied Palestinian Territories (www.ochaopt.org/content/barrier-gate-and-permit-regime-four-years-humanitarian-impact-northern-west-bank).

OCHA-oPT, United Nations Office for the Coordination of Humanitarian Affairs - Occupied Palestinian Territory, Mar. 2014, "Approaching the tenth anniversary of the ICJ advisory opinion: Impact of the Barrier on agricultural productivity in the northern West Bank", OCHA Occupied Palestinian Territories (www.ochaopt.org/content/approaching-tenth-anniversary-icj-advisory-opinion-impact-barrier-agricultural-0).

Pappé, Ilan, 2006, *The ethnic cleansing of Palestine*. Oxford, Oneworld.

Pfaffenberger, Bryan, Jun. 1988, "Fetishised Objects and Humanised Nature: Towards an Anthropology of Technology", *Man*, vol. 23, no. 2, 236–252 (www.jstor.org/stable/2802804).

Picard, Elizabeth, 1993, "Aux confins arabo-turcs: territoires, sécurité et ressources hydrauliques", in *La nouvelle dynamique au Moyen-Orient: Les relations entre l'Orient arabe et la Turquie*, Paris, L'Harmattan, 155–173. Comprendre le Moyen-Orient.

Pritchard, Sara B., 2011, *Confluence: the nature of technology and the remaking of the Rhône*. Cambridge, MA, Harvard University Press.

Rieu-Clarke, Alistair, Ruby Moynihan and Bjørn-Oliver Magsig, 2012, *UN watercourses convention user's guide*. Dundee, Scotland, IHP-HELP Centre for Water Law, Policy and Science.

Robins, Philip, Jun. 1997, "Turkish Foreign Policy under Erbakan", *Survival*, vol. 39, no. 2, 82–100 (www.tandfonline.com/doi/abs/10.1080/0039633970 8442913).

Rodríguez Echavarría, Tania, 2018, "Mitos y realidades de la gobernanza del agua en la cuenca transfronteriza del río Sixaola (Costa Rica-Panamá)", in Edith Kauffer, ed., *Cuencas transfronterizas: la apertura de la presa del nacionalismo metodológico*, Mexico, Centro de Investigación y Estudios Superiores en Antropología Social (CIESAS), 289–321. Biblioteca del agua.

Ross, Dennis, Jun 2011, *The missing peace: the inside story of the fight for Middle East peace*. epub ed., Farrar, Straus and Giroux.

Rowley, Gwyn, 2000, "Political Controls of River Waters and Abstractions between various States within the Middle East: Laws and Operations, with

Special Reference to the Jordan Basin", in Hussein Amery and Aaron T. Wolf, eds., *A geography of peace: water in the Middle East*, Austin, Texas University Press, 218–244.

Said, Edward W, 2016, *Orientalism: Western conceptions of the Orient*. London, Penguin.

Salman, Salman M. A., 2009, *The World Bank policy for projects on international waterways: an historical and legal analysis*. Washington, DC, World Bank (http://documents1.worldbank.org/curated/en/276451468325130824/pdf/487410PUB0inte101Official0Use0Only1.pdf). Law, justice, and development series.

Samaniego, Marco Antonio, 2006, *Ríos internacionales entre México y Estados Unidos: los tratados de 1906 y 1944*. Mexico, El Colegio de México.

Schleifer, Yigal, 4 Jun. 2008, "Turkey: dam project fosters development strategy debate", Eurasianet.org (www.eurasianet.org/departments/insight/articles/eav060408a.shtml).

Seale, Patrick, 1995, *Asad: the struggle for the Middle East*. Berkeley, University of California Press.

Seckler, David, Upali Amarasinghe, David Molden, Radhika De Silva and Randolph Baker, 1998, *World water demand and supply, 1990-2025: scenarios and issues*. Colombo, International Water Management Institute. Research Reports, 19.

Selby, Jan, 2003, *Water, power and politics in the Middle East: the other Israeli-Palestinian conflict*. London, I.B. Tauris. No. 25 in Library of modern Middle East studies.

Selby, Jan, Mar. 2005, "The Geopolitics of Water in the Middle East: Fantasies and Realities", *Third World Quarterly*, vol. 26, no. 2, 329–349 (https://doi.org/10.1080/0143659042000339146).

Selby, Jan, 2007, "Beyond Hydro-Hegemony: Gramsci, the National, and the Trans-National", in *Third International Workshop on Hydro-Hegemony, London School of Economics*, London.

Sezgin, Yuksel, 2002, "The October 1998 Crisis in Turkish-Syrian Relations: A Prospect Theory Approach", *Turkish Studies*, vol. 3, no. 2, 44–68.

Shapland, Greg, 1997, *Rivers of discord: international water disputes in the Middle East*. New York, St. Martin's Press.

Shuval, Hillel, 1996, "Towards Resolving Conflicts over Water between Israel and Its Neighbours", in John Anthony Allan ed., *Water, peace and the Middle East: negotiating resources in the Jordan Basin*, London, I.B. Tauris, 137–167. Library of Modern Middle East Studies, 9.

Singh, K. Gajendra, 14 Apr. 2005, "A new age for Turkey-Syria relations", *Asia Times Online* (www.atimes.com/atimes/Middle\s\do6(F)ast/GD14Ak01 html).

Smith, Jason Scott, 2009, *Building New Deal liberalism: the political economy of public works, 1933-1956*. New York, Cambridge University Press.

Smith, Neil, 2008, *Uneven development: nature, capital, and the production of space*. 3rd ed., Athens, Georgia, USA, University of Georgia Press.

Sneddon, Chris and Coleen Fox, Feb. 2006, "Rethinking Transboundary Waters: A Critical Hydropolitics of the Mekong Basin", *Political Geography*, vol. 25, no. 2, 181–202 (www.sciencedirect.com/science/article/abs/pii/S096262980 5001125).

Soffer, Arnon, 1999, *Rivers of fire: the conflict over water in the Middle East*. Lanham, Rowman & Littlefield, trans. from Hebrew by Arnon Rosovsky, Murray Copaken and Nina Soffer.

Soleimani, Kamal and Ahmad Mohammadpour, May 2022, "Las políticas de desdesarrollo en Kurdistán y Palestina", *Estudios de Asia y África*, vol. 57, no. 2, 249–288.

Staff, Toi, 22 Nov. 2021, "Israel, Jordan sign huge UAE-brokered deal to swap solar energy and water", The Times of Israel (www.timesofisrael.com/israel-jordan-sign-uae-brokered-deal-to-swap-solar-energy-and-water/).

Starr, Joyce S., 1995, *Covenant over Middle Eastern waters: key to world survival*. New York, Henry Holt.

Steinberg, Theodore, Apr. 1993, "'That Worlds Fair Feeling': Control of Water in 20th-Century America", *Technology and Culture*, vol. 34, no. 2, 401–409 (www.jstor.org/stable/3106543).

Stergiou, Dimitrios, May 2016, "ISIS Political Economy: Financing a Terror State", *Journal of Money Laundering Control*, vol. 19, no. 2, 189–207.

Tal, Alon, 2017, *The land is full: addressing overpopulation in Israel*. Yale University Press.

Talozi, Samer, Amelia Altz-Stamm, Hussam Hussein and Peter Reich, May 2019, "What Constitutes an Equitable Water Share? A Reassessment of Equitable Apportionment in the Jordan–Israel Water Agreement 25 Years Later", *Water Policy*, vol. 21, no. 5, 911–933.

The Zionist Organization, 3 Feb. 1919, *Statement of the Zionist Organization regarding Palestine* (http://unispal.un.org/UNISPAL.NSF/0/2D1C045FB C3F12688525704B006F29CC).

Toussaint, Eric, 2022, *Banco Mundial: una historia crítica*. Barcelona, El Viejo Topo, trans. from French by Griselda Piñero.

Traverso, Enzo, 2012, *L'histoire comme champ de bataille: interpréter les violences du XXe siècle*. Paris, La Découverte.

Tripp, Charles, 2002, *A history of Iraq*. 2nd ed., Cambridge, Cambridge University Press.

Turkish Republic, Ministry of Foreign Affairs, 4 Jul. 2014, "Press release regarding the amount of water that turkey releases from the Euphrates River", T.R. MFA (www.mfa.gov.tr/no_-228_-4-july-2014_-press-release-regarding-the-amount-of-water-that-turkey-releases-from-the-euphrates-river.en.mfa).

Turkish Republic, Ministry of Foreign Affairs, Department of Regional and Transboundary Waters, 1996, "Water Issues between Turkey, Syria and Iraq", *Perceptions: Journal of International Affairs*, vol. 1, no. 3, 0–14 (https://dergipark.org.tr/en/pub/perception/issue/49044/625645).

Turkish Republic, Ministry of Foreign Affairs, Department of Regional and Transboundary Waters, 1997, *Water: A Source of Conflict of Coopeariton in the Middle East?*, Turkish Ministry of Foreign Affairs (www.mfa.gov.tr/data/ DISPOLITIKA/WaterASourceofConflictofCoopintheMiddleEast.pdf).

Turton, Anthony, 2002, "Hydropolitics: the Concept and Its Limitations", in *Hydropolitics in the Developing World: A Southern African Perspective*, Pretoria, African Water Issues Research Unit, University of Pretoria, 13–19.

von Hein, Shabnam, Jul. 2021, "Iran: Drought, water shortages spark protests", Deutsche Welle (www.dw.com/en/iran-drought-water-shortages-spark-prote sts/a-58651779).

Ward, Diane Raines, 2002, *Water wars: drought, flood, folly, and the politics of thirst*. New York, Riverhead Books.

Warner, Jeroen, 2004, "Plugging the GAP – Working with Buzan: The Ilısu Dam as a Security Issue", in *SOAS Water Issues Study Group Occasional Paper*, no. 67.

Warner, Jeroen, 2008, "Contested Hydrohegemony: Hydraulic Control and Security in Turkey", *Water Alternatives*, vol. 1, no. 2, 271–288 (www.wateralternatives.org/index.php/volume1/v1issue2/32-a1-2-6/file).

Warner, Jeroen, 2010, "Hydro-Hegemonic Politics: A Crossroads on the Euphrates-Tigris?", in Kai Wegerich and Jeroen Warner, eds., *The politics of water: a survey*, London, Routledge, 119–141.

Warner, Jeroen, Mark Zeitoun and Naho Mirumachi, Jun. 2013, "How 'Soft Power' Shapes Transboundary Water Interaction", in *GWF Discussion Paper 1323*, Global Water Forum (www.globalwaterforum.org/2013/06/03/6928/).

Waterbury, John, 1979, *Hydropolitics of the Nile Valley*. New York, Syracuse University Press. Contemporary Issues in the Middle East.

Wheeler, Kevin G. and Hussam Hussein, Oct. 2021, "Water Research and Nationalism in the Post-Truth Era", *Water International*, 1–8 (www.tandfonl ine.com/doi/full/10.1080/02508060.2021.1986942).

Wilson, Nicole J., Teresa Montoya, Rachel Arseneault and Andrew Curley, Jun. 2021, "Governing Water Insecurity: Navigating Indigenous Water Rights and Regulatory Politics in Settler Colonial States", *Water International*, vol. 46, no. 6, 783–801 (www.tandfonline.com/doi/full/10.1080/02508060. 2021.1928972).

Wolf, Aaron T., 1994, "A Hydropolitical History of the Nile, Jordan, and Euphrates River Basins", in Asit K. Biswas, ed., *International waters of the Middle East*, Oxford, Oxford University Press, 5–43.

Wolf, Aaron T., 1995, *Hydropolitics along the Jordan River: scarce water and its impact on the Arab-Israeli conflict*. Tokyo, United Nations University Press.

Wolf, Aaron T., 2000, "'Hydrostrategic Territory' in the Jordan Basin: Water, War, and Arab-Israeli Peace Negotiations", in Hussein Amery and Aaron T. Wolf, eds., *A geography of peace: water in the Middle East*, Austin, Texas University Press, 63–120.

Woodhouse, Melvin and Mark Zeitoun, 2008, "Hydro-Hegemony and International Water Law: Grappling with the Gaps of Power and Law", *Water Policy*, vol. 10, Supplement 2, 103–119.

Yalqiyian, Michael, 25 Sep. 2015, "'Dā'ish' wa-l-Sirā' 'ala-l-Miyāh fi Sūriya wa-l-'Irāq", Beirut Center for Middle East Studies (www.beirutme.com/? p=3187).

Zeitoun, Mark, 2011, *Power and water in the Middle East: the hidden politics of the Palestinian-Israeli water conflict.* 2nd ed., London, I.B. Tauris.

Zeitoun, Mark, Ana Elisa Cascão, Jeroen Warner, Naho Mirumachi, Nathanial Matthews, Filippo Menga and Rebecca Farnum, 2017, "Transboundary Water Interaction III: Contesting Hegemonic Arrangements", *International Environmental Agreements: Politics, Law and Economics*, vol. 17, no. 2, 271–294 (http://dx.doi.org/10.1007/s10784-016-9325-x).

Zeitoun, Mark and Naho Mirumachi, 2008, "Transboundary Water Interaction I: Reconsidering Conflict and Cooperation", *International Environmental Agreements: Politics, Law and Economics*, vol. 8, no. 4, 297–316.

Zeitoun, Mark, Naho Mirumachi and Jeroen Warner, 2011, "Transboundary Water Interaction II: The Influence of 'Soft' Power", *International Environmental Agreements: Politics, Law and Economics*, vol. 11, no. 2, 159–178 (http://dx.doi.org/10.1007/s10784-010-9134-6).

Zeitoun, Mark and Jeroen Warner, 2006, "Hydro-Hegemony – A Framework for Analysis of Trans-Boundary Water Conflicts", *Water Policy*, vol. 8, 435–460.

Özhan, Taha, Jul. 2008, "New action plan for southeastern Turkey", SETA Policy Brief, no. 18 (https://ciaotest.cc.columbia.edu/wps/seta/0001592/f_0001592_805.pdf).

Ünver, I.H. Olcay, 1997, "Southeastern Anatolia Project (GAP)", *International Journal of Water Resources Development*, vol. 13, no. 4, 453–484.

Index

For Product Safety Concerns and Information please contact our EU
representative GPSR@taylorandfrancis.com
Taylor & Francis Verlag GmbH, Kaufingerstraße 24, 80331 München, Germany

www.ingramcontent.com/pod-product-compliance
Lightning Source LLC
Chambersburg PA
CBHW061749270326
41928CB00011B/2439